SMP 11-16

Book B4

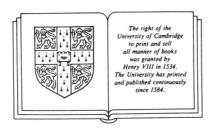
Cambridge University Press

Cambridge
New York   New Rochelle   Melbourne   Sydney

Published by the Press Syndicate of the University of Cambridge
The Pitt Building, Trumpington Street, Cambridge CB2 1RP
32 East 57th Street, New York, NY 10022, USA
10 Stamford Road, Oakleigh, Melbourne 3166, Australia

First published 1987
Third printing 1989

Illustrations by David Parkins and Chris Evans
Photographs by John Ling
Typesetting and diagrams by Parkway Group, London and
Abingdon, and Gecko Limited, Bicester, Oxon
Cover photograph by Graham Portlock

Printed in Great Britain by Scotprint, Musselburgh, Scotland

British Library cataloguing in publication data

SMP 11–16 blue series.
  Bk B4
  1. Mathematics – 1961–
  I. School Mathematics Project
  510   QA39.2
  ISBN 0 521 31469 0

Acknowledgements
The authors and the publisher would like to thank the following
for permission to use copyright material: A. F. Kersting (p. 12
left). Stanley Freese (p. 12 centre and right), Daimler Benz AG
(p. 13 top), Italeri (pp. 13–15), Mick Moore (p. 53 left),
Tucktonia Ltd. (p. 61 top).

Contents

1 Using a calculator

A Order of operations

Look at this calculation: $2 + 5 \times 3 =$

It can mean two different things. We could do $2 + 5$ first, or we could do 5×3 first.

We can use **brackets** to show the two different ways to do the calculation.

Doing $2 + 3$ first	**Doing 5×3 first**
$(2 + 5) \times 3$	$2 + (5 \times 3)$
$7 \quad \times 3 = 21$	$2 + \quad 15 = 17$

A1 Work out   (a) $5 + (3 \times 4)$ (b) $(5 + 3) \times 4$

A2 (a) Write down $6 + 2 \times 5$.
   Now put brackets into the calculation to make the answer come to 16.

   (b) Write down $6 + 2 \times 5$ again.
   This time put brackets into the calculation to make the answer come to 40.

A3 (a) Write down $6 + 12 \div 3$. Put in brackets to make the answer come to 10.

   (b) Write down $6 + 12 \div 3$ again. Put in brackets to make the answer come to 6.

A4 What different answers can you get to this calculation by putting brackets in different places: $20 - 6 \div 2$

A5 What different answers can you get to this calculation by putting brackets in different places: $15 \div 3 + 2$

A6 Imagine that you have seven cards printed like this:

   You can arrange them in different ways to make calculations.
   For example you could have $3 + (5 \times 4)$, which comes to 23.
   (a) Can you arrange them to get an answer of   (i) 27   (ii) 32   (iii) 17
   (b) What other answers can you get?

B Two different types of calculator

We have seen that $2 + 5 \times 3$ can mean two different things.
It depends which operation you do first, the $+$ or the $\times$.

What happens if you do it on a calculator, like this?

$$\boxed{2}\ \boxed{+}\ \boxed{5}\ \boxed{\times}\ \boxed{3}\ \boxed{=}$$

The answer depends on the type of calculator you have, because there
are two different types of calculator.

The first type we shall call the 'left-to-right' (LTR) type, because
it works through the calculation from left to right, like this:

$$2\ +\ 5\ \text{(That's 7 so far.)}\ \times\ 3\ \text{(That's 21.)}\ =\ \text{(Result 21)}$$

The second type of calculator automatically puts brackets round any
multiplications or **divisions**, and does them first.

If you key in $2 + 5 \times 3 =$, it will do $2 + (5 \times 3)$ and get 17.

We shall call this type of the MDF type ('multiplication and division first').

B1 Key in $2 + 5 \times 3 =$ on your calculator.
Which type, LTR or MDF, do you have?

B2 Write down what answer you think you will get when you key
this into your calculator: $3 + 4 \times 5 =$

Now do it on your calculator and check that you were right.

B3 Write down what answer you think you will get from your calculator
when you key in $4 + 12 \div 2 =$

Do it on your calculator and check you were right.

B4 What answer do you expect to get from your calculator for
$$8 - 3 \times 2 + 6 \div 2 =$$
Check that you are right.

B5 Write down the answer you expect to get from your calculator
for each of these. Then check you are right.

(a) $4 \times 3 - 2 \times 5 =$ (b) $9 - 2 \times 4 + 5 =$
(c) $10 - 6 \div 2 =$ (d) $12 \div 3 + 6 \div 2 =$

C Calculations with brackets

Some calculators have brackets keys. These make it easy to do calculations containing brackets.

For example, if you want to do $8 \times (4 + 3)$ on a calculator with brackets keys, you just key in

[8] [×] [(] [4] [+] [3] [)] [=]

If your calculator does not have brackets keys, you have to be extra careful.

Read this if your calculator is an LTR type without brackets keys.

Do the part in brackets first, and press [=].
Then do the rest of the calculation.

Examples

$8 \times (4 + 3)$ Do $4 + 3$ first. Then multiply the result by 8.

[4] [+] [3] [=] [×] [8] [=]

$(9 + 7) \div 4$ Do $9 + 7$ first. Then divide the result by 4.

[9] [+] [7] [=] [÷] [4] [=]

$5 + (8 \div 2)$ Do $8 \div 2$ first. Then add 5 to the result.

[8] [÷] [2] [=] [+] [5] [=]

Read this if your calculator is an MDF type without brackets keys.

If the part in brackets is a $\times$ or a $\div$, the calculator will put the brackets in automatically.

If the part in brackets is a $+$ or a $-$, then do this part first and press [=]. Then do the rest of the calculation.

Examples

$8 \times (4 + 3)$ Do $4 + 3$ first. Press [=]. Then multiply by 8.

[4] [+] [3] [=] [×] [8] [=]

$(9 + 7) \div 4$ Do $9 + 7$ first. Press [=]. Then divide by 4.

[9] [+] [7] [=] [÷] [4] [=]

$5 + (8 \div 2)$ Brackets will be inserted round $8 \div 2$ automatically.

[5] [+] [8] [÷] [2] [=]

C1   Do these on your calculator. Then do them in your head and check that your calculator method was right.

(a) $4 \times (3 + 2)$ (b) $6 \times (3 + 1)$ (c) $3 + (8 \div 4)$
(d) $(3 + 7) \times 2$ (e) $(5 + 7) \div 3$ (f) $10 + (3 \times 2)$

C2 Use your calculator to work out each of these.

(a) 26 + (38 × 15) (b) (26 + 38) × 15 (c) 48 + (128 ÷ 16)

(d) (48 + 128) ÷ 16 (e) (117 + 78) ÷ 13 (f) 117 + (78 ÷ 13)

The answers are at the bottom of page 5.

C3 Do these on your calculator.

(a) 18·3 + (4·2 × 1·5) (b) 6·5 × (2·7 + 3·9) (c) 15·8 + (10·2 ÷ 1·5)

(d) (7·3 + 1·8) × 2·4 (e) (10·4 − 2·6) ÷ 1·3 (f) 2·7 × (3·8 − 1·3)

Now check your answers. The correct answers are at the bottom of page 6.

Division

The 'horizontal bar' sign for division acts like brackets in a calculation.

For example

$3 + \dfrac{8}{2}$ means $3 + (8 \div 2)$ $\qquad$ $\dfrac{7 + 2}{3}$ means $(7 + 2) \div 3$

If you have brackets keys, both of these calculations are easy.

If you do not have brackets keys, you have to be careful.
Here is how to do these calculations on the two different types of calculator, without brackets keys. Read whichever applies to you.

$3 + \dfrac{8}{2}$ $\quad$ Do 8 ÷ 2 first and press $\boxed{=}$. $\qquad$ $\boxed{8}\ \boxed{÷}\ \boxed{2}\ \boxed{=}\ \boxed{+}\ \boxed{3}\ \boxed{=}$
$\qquad\qquad$ Then add 3.

$\dfrac{7 + 2}{3}$ $\quad$ Do 7 + 2 first and press $\boxed{=}$. $\qquad$ $\boxed{7}\ \boxed{+}\ \boxed{2}\ \boxed{=}\ \boxed{÷}\ \boxed{3}\ \boxed{=}$
$\qquad\qquad$ Then divide by 3.

$3 + \dfrac{8}{2}$ $\quad$ Brackets will be inserted $\qquad$ $\boxed{3}\ \boxed{+}\ \boxed{8}\ \boxed{÷}\ \boxed{2}\ \boxed{=}$
$\qquad\qquad$ round 8 ÷ 2 automatically.

$\dfrac{7 + 2}{3}$ $\quad$ Do 7 + 2 first. Press $\boxed{=}$. $\qquad$ $\boxed{7}\ \boxed{+}\ \boxed{2}\ \boxed{=}\ \boxed{÷}\ \boxed{3}\ \boxed{=}$
$\qquad\qquad$ Then divide by 3.

C4 (a) Do $\dfrac{8 + 12}{4}$ on your calculator. Then do it in your head

and check that your calculator method was right.

(b) Do the same for $8 + \dfrac{12}{4}$.

4

C5 Do these on your calculator. Check your calculator method by doing the calculations in your head.

(a) $4 + \dfrac{6}{2}$ (b) $\dfrac{4 + 6}{2}$ (c) $\dfrac{12 - 4}{2}$ (d) $\dfrac{12}{2} - 4$

C6 Do these on your calculator.

(a) $43 + \dfrac{105}{7}$ (b) $\dfrac{286}{13} - 14$ (c) $\dfrac{483 - 218}{53}$

(d) $\dfrac{384}{48} + 26$ (e) $117 + \dfrac{576}{96}$ (f) $\dfrac{470 - 198}{34}$

D Using formulas

Worked example

The formula $v = u + at$ is used in science.
Use the formula to work out v when u is $34 \cdot 5$, a is $7 \cdot 2$ and t is 55.

Start by writing down the formula. $\longrightarrow$ $v = u + at$

Replace u, a and t by their values.
Write down the calculation you have to do. $\longrightarrow$ $v = 34 \cdot 5 + (7 \cdot 2 \times 55)$

Notice the **brackets** to show that $7 \cdot 2 \times 55$ has to be done first.

Now think how to do it on your calculator. $\qquad v = 430 \cdot 5$

D1 Temperatures in degrees Celsius (°C) can be converted to degrees Fahrenheit (°F) by using this formula:

$f = 32 + 1 \cdot 8c$

c stands for the temperature in °C.
f stands for the temperature in °F.

Convert these temperatures to degrees Fahrenheit.
(a) 10°C   (b) 23°C   (c) 85°C   (d) 36·9°C

D2 Use the formula $y = a + bx$ to calculate y when

(a) $a = 15$, $b = 3$ and $x = 10$

(b) $a = 14 \cdot 4$, $b = 0 \cdot 8$ and $x = 7 \cdot 5$

Answers to question C2: (a) 596 (b) 960 (c) 56 (d) 11 (e) 15 (f) 123

D3 The length of this spring depends on the weight hanging on the end of it.

The formula connecting the length and the weight is

$$l = 37\cdot5 + \frac{w}{2\cdot5}$$

l is the length of the spring, in cm.
w is the weight on the end, in kg.

(a) Calculate l when w is 17·5.

(b) Calculate l when w is 24·0.

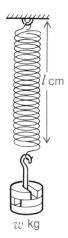

E A cross-figure

Copy the diagram.
Do not write on this page.

Clues across

1 $79 + (17 \times 18)$

3 $\dfrac{948 + 846}{78}$

4 $6 \times (138 + 439)$

7 $88 + (53 \times 45)$

9 When 1 across is divided by this number, the answer is 11.

10 $577 + \dfrac{1652}{59}$

Clues down

1 $(44 + 27) \times (33 + 19)$

2 $91 +$ twice 7 across

3 $\dfrac{4004}{14} - 50$

5 $(89 + 68) \times 28$

6 3 across multiplied by 95

8 $368 + \dfrac{893}{19}$

Answers to question C3: (a) 24·6 (b) 42·9 (c) 22·6 (d) 21·84 (e) 6 (f) 6·75

2 In your head (1)

Do these in your head, as quickly as you can.

1 (a) 4×5　　(b) 7×3　　(c) 6×6　　(d) 5×8　　(e) 7×7

2 (a) $28 + 5$　　(b) $36 + 7$　　(c) $45 + 9$　　(d) $88 + 8$　　(e) $6 + 28$

3 (a) $43 + 25$　　(b) $57 + 38$　　(c) $36 + 19$　　(d) $44 + 17$　　(e) $28 + 52$

4 (a) $54 - 3$　　(b) $36 - 8$　　(c) $27 - 9$　　(d) $81 - 7$　　(e) $42 - 5$

5 (a) $27 - 14$　　(b) $51 - 18$　　(c) $33 - 28$　　(d) $85 - 36$　　(e) $72 - 27$

6 Write each of these fractions as a decimal.

   (a) $\frac{3}{4}$　(b) $\frac{7}{10}$　(c) $\frac{2}{5}$　(d) $\frac{73}{100}$　(e) $\frac{9}{100}$

7 Work these out.

   (a) $\frac{1}{3}$ of 12　(b) $\frac{1}{4}$ of 24　(c) $\frac{1}{6}$ of 36　(d) $\frac{1}{5}$ of 40　(e) $\frac{1}{2}$ of 46

8 (a) $\frac{2}{3}$ of 18　(b) $\frac{3}{4}$ of 16　(c) $\frac{3}{5}$ of 25　(d) $\frac{5}{8}$ of 24　(e) $\frac{4}{5}$ of 45

9 Multiply each of these numbers by 10.

   (a) 15　(b) 16·3　(c) 7·34　(d) 0·09　(e) 0·84

10 How much change do you get from £1 if you spend

   (a) 47p　(b) 18p　(c) 66p　(d) 71p　(e) 23p

11 How much change do you get from £5 if you spend

   (a) £4·80　(b) £1·60　(c) £0·20　(d) £3·30　(e) £2·70

12 3 people share £2·40 equally. How much does each get?

13 7 people each give 40p towards a birthday present for a friend. How much is that altogether?

14 I have to be at the airport at 9:15. The time now is 8:40. How long have I got?

15 Change these measurements to metres.

   (a) 183 cm　(b) 42 cm　(c) 260 cm　(d) 7 cm　(e) 130·5 cm

3 Views

A What do you see?

A1 Jane serves Jim with three mugs of tea.
She puts them on the counter like this.

(a) Which of these pictures show the mugs as Jim sees them?

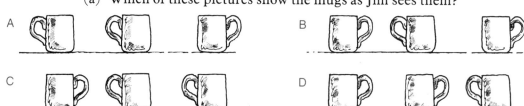

A   B

C   D

(b) Jim takes the empty mugs back
to the counter. He puts them
on the counter like this.

Draw the mugs as Jane sees them.

A2 Sally sits opposite Darren at dinner.
She puts a salt pot, a pepper pot and
a knife and fork in front of her,
like this.

Which of the pictures below
shows what Darren sees?

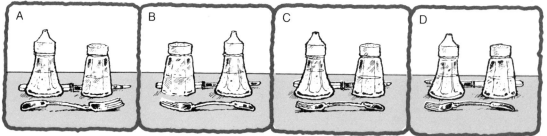

A   B   C   D

A3 Paul, Qahir, Rosie and Sarah are looking at a model house.

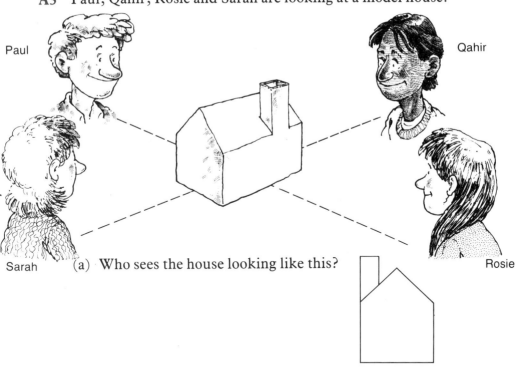

(a) Who sees the house looking like this?

(b) Who sees it like this?

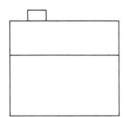

(c) Jane comes to look at the house. She stands between two of the people already there.

To Jane the house looks like this.

Between which two people is she standing?

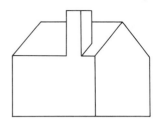

(d) Jane moves to a new position. From her new position the house looks like this.

Between which two people is she standing now?

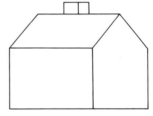

An **aerial view** is a picture taken from the air. It could be taken from a plane or a helicopter, for example.

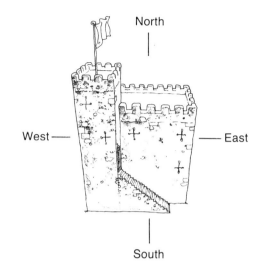

A4 The picture on the right is an aerial view of a castle, taken from the south.

From which direction was each of these aerial views taken?

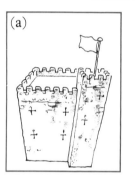

(a)

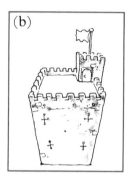

(b)

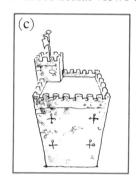

(c)

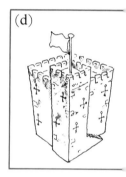

(d)

B Views – front, back, side and top

This is a photo of a 1938 Mercedes Benz W154.

You can see some detail in the photo, but other things cannot be seen. For example, you cannot see what shape the back of the car is.

10

Imagine the car is put into a glass box.

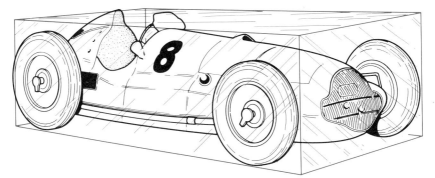

When you look straight at the front of the box, you get this view. It is called the **front view**.

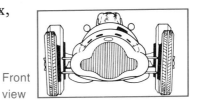

Front
view

If you look straight at the side of the box, you see a **side view**.

Side
view

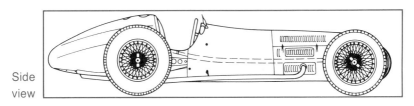

In the same way, this is the **back view**.

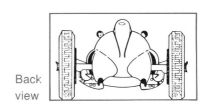

Back
view

This is the **top view**, often called the **plan view**.

Plan
view

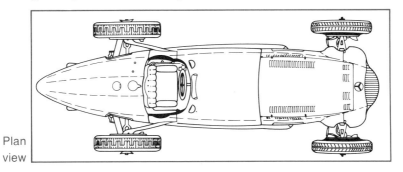

B1 Which view shows most clearly that the front tyres are smaller than the rear tyres?

11

Pakenham Mill Headcorn Mill Worlingworth Mill

B2 These are photos of three old windmills.
There are views of the windmills below.
Which view goes with which windmill?

Write your answers like this: A is the plan view of Pakenham.

C Diagrams in use: a model car kit

This is a Mercedes 540K.

You can buy a plastic kit to make a model of the car.
Diagrams and photos come with the kit.

Here are three views of the car.

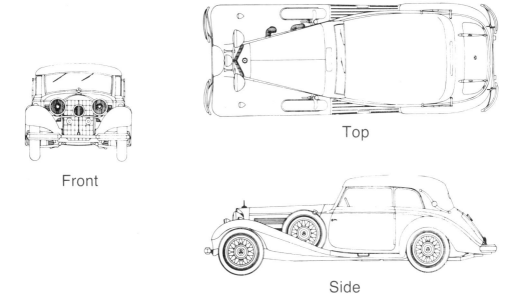

Top

Front

Side

C1 (a) The car has two spare wheels. Which view shows
          both of them most clearly?

    (b) In which views can you see the windscreen wipers?

C2 The real car is about 5 m long. Roughly how wide and how high
    is it?

Each part in the kit has a number.
There are diagrams in the kit to help you tell which part is which.

The diagram on the opposite page is called an **exploded diagram**.
It tells you how some of the parts fit together.

C3 In the kit there are six parts which have the number 58.
Find part number 58 in the exploded diagram.

(a) What is part number 58?

(b) Why are there six of them in the kit?

C4 Here is a picture of one of the spare wheels.

(a) How many parts is it made from?

(b) What are the numbers of the parts?

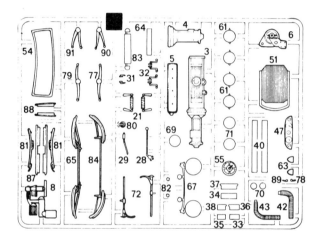

C5 Here are some of the parts that come in the kit. All these parts are coloured silver.

(a) How many parts have the number 63?

(b) Find them on the exploded diagram. What do you think they are?

C6 (a) What does part number 78 fix into?

(b) What is the number of the same part on the other side of the model?

C7 Find parts 67 and 80.

(a) When the model is finished, which of these parts is nearer to the front of the car?

(b) Which one is nearer to the ground?

C8 (a) Find part 67 on the exploded diagram.
How many other parts fix onto part 67?

(b) How many of these parts are definitely silver-coloured?

C9 Part 75 is the back window. It is clear – you can see through it.
What are the numbers of other parts that you think are clear?

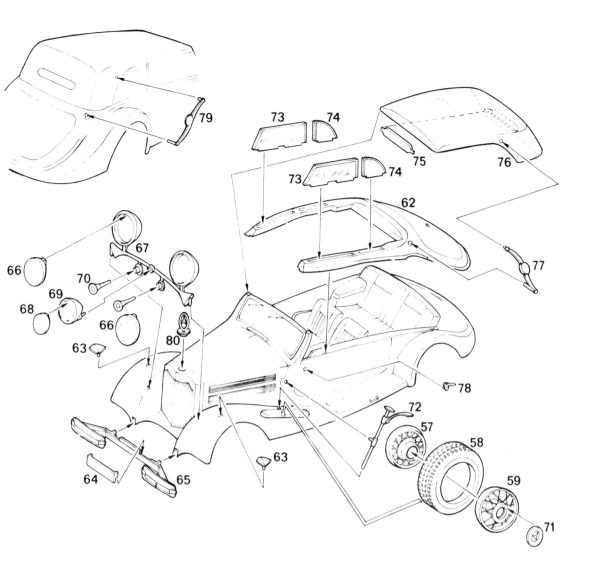

79

73 74

73 74

75 76

62

66 67 77

70

69 68 66 78

63 80

64 65 63 72 57 58 59 71

4 Time

A Time calculations: a review

Worked example (1)

How long is it from 10:35 to 12:15?

Think of a 'time line'.

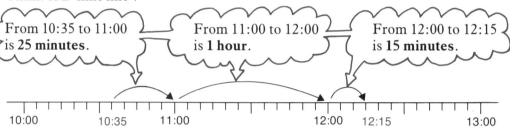

That's **1 hour 40 minutes** altogether.

> **A1** How long is it from (a) 06:40 to 07:05 (b) 09:50 to 11:20
> (c) 07:45 to 10:10 (d) 08:25 to 10:15 (e) 14:35 to 16:10

Worked example (2)

How long is it from 08:15 to 10:40?

Here are two methods.

Method 1

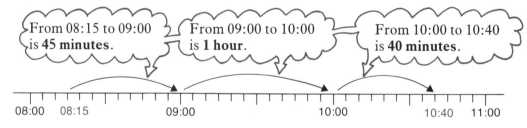

That's 1 hour and 85 minutes altogether.
But 85 minutes = 1 hour and 25 minutes.
So altogether it's **2 hours and 25 minutes**.

Method 2

From 08:15 to 10:15 is **2 hours**. From 10:15 to 10:40 is **25 minutes**.

That's **2 hours 25 minutes** altogether.

A2 How long is it from (a) 06:05 to 08:50 (b) 09:15 to 11:50
(c) 07:20 to 11:55 (d) 13:10 to 16:05 (e) 17:35 to 19:20

Worked example (3)

A coach journey takes $1\frac{3}{4}$ hours. The coach starts out at 08:40.
When does it reach its destination?

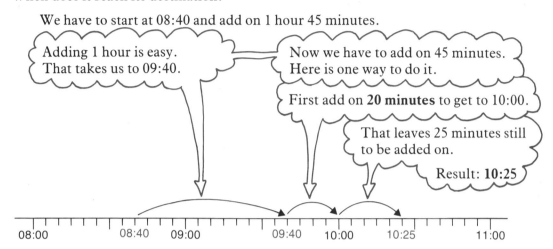

We have to start at 08:40 and add on 1 hour 45 minutes.

Adding 1 hour is easy.
That takes us to 09:40.

Now we have to add on 45 minutes.
Here is one way to do it.

First add on **20 minutes** to get to 10:00.

That leaves 25 minutes still
to be added on.

Result: **10:25**

08:00   08:40   09:00   09:40   10:00   10:25   11:00

A3 A film lasts for 2 hours 20 minutes.
The film starts at 7:50 p.m. At what time will it finish?

A4 Karl has a joint of meat which will take $2\frac{3}{4}$ hours to cook.
He puts it in the oven at 10:35 a.m. At what time will it
be finished?

A5 Wendy is going to fly a light aircraft from Southend to Edinburgh.
She estimates that the journey will take $3\frac{1}{2}$ hours.

She takes off at 04:40. What is her estimated time of arrival
at Edinburgh?

A6 The first performance of a school play was an afternoon performance.
It started at 2 p.m. and ended at 4:25 p.m.

(a) How long did the play last?

(b) Evening performances of the play start at 7:45 p.m.
At what time will they end?

A7 A ferry takes 3 hours 40 minutes to cross the Channel from Dover
to Ostend. What are the arrival times of ferries leaving Dover at

(a) 0615 (b) 0805 (c) 0925 (d) 1050

DELAY

You need a dice and worksheet B4–1.

You are a special agent working in Glasgow.

These instructions arrive.

You must go to Morecambe. Then you have to go to Dover and catch a ferry or hovercraft to France.

But trains are always delayed . . .

URGENT

Travel by train to Morecambe.
Collect message in buffet.
Then to Dover and France.
Change trains often.
Rudolph.

Remember

1　You start on the 7:10 from Glasgow. This **should** arrive in Lancaster at 9:29.
But . . .
trains in this game are always late!

2　This is how to find out how late a train will be between two towns.

Throw the dice.
Multiply the dice score by the number in the circle between the two towns.

This tells you how many minutes late the train will be in arriving.

3　Use the timetables to decide which trains to catch.

4　You **must** go to Morecambe.

5　It takes you exactly 1 hour to get from London Euston to Charing Cross.

6　It takes you exactly 20 minutes from Dover station to get to either the ferry port or the hover port.

7　Fill in the worksheet as you go.

8　The person who leaves the country earliest is the winner!

Station	Timetable arrival time	Real arrival time	Departure time
Glasgow			0710
Lancaster	9:29	10:19	10:45
Morecambe	10:55		
Lancaster			
Crewe			
Birmingham			

Here is the start of Karen's journey. She catches the 7:10 from Glasgow. This should arrive at Lancaster at 9:29.

She throws the dice and gets 5. So her train is 50 minutes late. She gets to Lancaster at 10:19.

From the timetable, the next train to Morecambe departs at 10:45.

This should arrive at 10:55, and so on.

dep. Glasgow Central	07 10	07 23	08 23	10 10	11 15	12 10	13 23	15 23	17 10	18 23
arr. Lancaster	09 29	09 49	10 57	12 28	13 48	14 27	15 53	17 57	19 29	21 02

dep. Lancaster	08 39	09 35	10 45	11 20	11 33	12 01	13 53	14 32	15 21
arr. Morecambe	08 49	09 45	10 55	11 30	11 46	12 11	14 03	14 42	15 31
dep. Morecambe	08 55	10 10	11 05	11 40	12 26	13 10	14 08	15 05	15 45
arr. Lancaster	09 05	10 20	11 15	11 50	12 36	13 21	14 18	15 16	15 57

dep. Lancaster	arr. Crewe
09 49	10 59
10 29	11 42
12 28	14 06
13 48	14 56
14 27	15 37
15 53	17 00
17 50	18 01
19 29	20 35

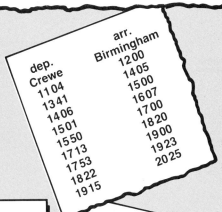

dep. Crewe	arr. Birmingham
11 04	12 00
13 41	14 05
14 06	15 00
15 01	16 07
15 50	17 00
17 13	18 20
17 53	19 00
18 22	19 23
19 15	20 25

Birmingham (New Street) to London Euston

dep. B'ham	arr. Euston			dep. B'ham	arr. Euston		
11 48	13 33	☕	✗	16 18	18 00	☕	✗
12 18	14 05	☕	✗	16 48	18 30	☕	✗
12 48	14 33	☕	✗	17 18	18 58		
13 18	15 05	☕	✗	17 48	19 31	☕	
13 48	15 33	☕	✗	18 18	20 03		
14 18	16 05	☕	✗	18 48	20 28		
14 48	16 33	☕	✗	19 29	21 11	☕	✗
15 18	17 02	☕		20 03	21 43	☕	
15 48	17 36	☕	✗	21 48	23 29		

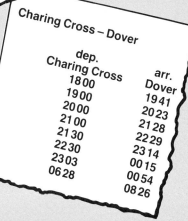

dep. Charing Cross	arr. Dover
18 00	19 41
19 00	20 23
20 00	21 28
21 00	22 29
21 30	23 14
22 30	00 15
23 03	00 54
06 28	08 26

DOVER FERRY PORT
Sailings to France
1905
2030
2110
2200
2250
2340
0115
0605
0800
0910

DOVER HOVER PORT
Hovercraft to France
depart 08 00
1000
1200
1400
1600
1800
2000

5 Probability

A Equally likely outcomes

Some things are **certain** to happen.

If you let go of a brick, 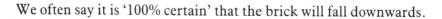 it will certainly fall downwards.

We often say it is '100% certain' that the brick will fall downwards.

Some things are not certain.

If you throw a coin, it may land 'head' or 'tail'.

If the coin is fair, then 'head' and 'tail' are **equally likely**.

We say the **probability** of getting a head is $\frac{1}{2}$ or 50%, and the probability of getting a tail is also 50%.

Probability is a way of measuring how **likely** something is.

Something whose probability is 0% never happens.

Something whose probability is 100% always happens.

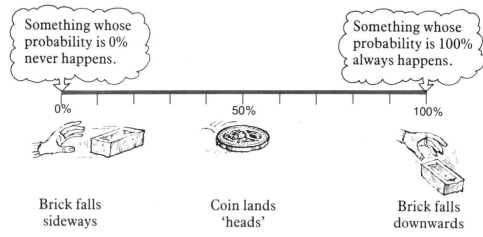

| Brick falls | Coin lands | Brick falls |
| sideways | 'heads' | downwards |

A1 Think of something whose probability of happening is

(a) 0%   (b) 100%   (c) very close to 100% but not quite 100%

(d) very close to 0% but not quite 0%

Sharon has 4 cards. They are the aces of hearts, diamonds, clubs and spades.	She shuffles the cards and holds them up. Her boyfriend Sam has to pick one card. He gets a kiss if he picks the ace of hearts.

How likely is it that Sam will pick the ace of hearts?
There are 4 cards. Any of them could be the ace of hearts.
Sam has a '1 in 4 chance' of picking the ace of hearts.

We say that the probability that he picks the ace of hearts is $\frac{1}{4}$, or 25%.

We often use **fractions** instead of percentages for probabilities, when the fractions are simple.

A2 A bag contains 10 balls. One of them is red and the others are all white.

The bag is shaken to mix up the balls. Someone puts her hand in the bag and takes out a ball without looking.

What is the probability that she takes out the red ball? Write the answer as a fraction.

A3 One of these cards is the queen of spades. Sally picks a card. What is the probability that she picks the queen of spades?

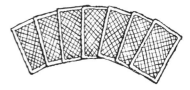

A4 Amin puts these cards **face down** on the table:
king of clubs, king of diamonds, queen of hearts, jack of clubs, ace of hearts, jack of hearts, ace of spades, king of spades.

He shuffles the cards and asks his friend to pick a card.

What is the probability that his friend picks the jack of clubs?

A5 A box contains 1 black counter and 14 white counters. Sandra shakes the box and takes out a counter without looking.

What is the probability that she takes out the black counter?

A6 Ray shakes a bag containing a red counter and 8 black counters. He takes out a counter without looking. What is the probability that he takes out the red counter?

B Comparing chances

B1 Imagine that you like red sweets but hate black ones.

These two bags are shaken up, and you take out a sweet from each bag without looking.

Which bag are you more likely to pick a red sweet from?

B2 In each part below, say which is more likely, and give your reasons. If you think the two things are equally likely, say so.

(a) Picking a red sweet from bag C, ... or picking a red sweet from bag D.

(b) Picking a red sweet from bag E, ... or picking a red sweet from bag F.

(c) Picking a red sweet from bag G, ... or picking a red sweet from bag H.

(d) Picking a red sweet from bag I, ... or picking a red sweet from bag J.

B3 A bag K contains 1 red sweet and 3 black sweets.
A bag L contains 2 red sweets and 7 black sweets.

Which is more likely, picking a red sweet from bag K or picking a red sweet from bag L?

B4 The contents of bags G and I above are emptied into a new bag M.
The contents of H and J are emptied into a new bag N.

Which is more likely, picking a red sweet from bag M, or picking a red sweet from bag N?

c Calculating probabilities

Sam puts 2 red counters and 3 black counters into a bag. He shakes them out.

Sharon picks a counter without looking. She gets a kiss if the counter is red.

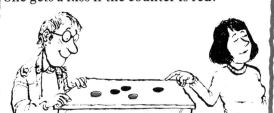

There are 5 counters for Sharon to pick from. 2 of them are red. So Sharon has a '2 in 5 chance' of picking a red counter.

The probability that Sharon picks a red counter is $\frac{2}{5}$.

C1 What is the probability that Sharon in the picture above will pick a black counter?

C2 Ranjit has these 8 cards.   She shuffles them and puts them face down.

If you pick up a card, what is the probability that you will pick
(a) a red card   (b) a black card

C3 Ivan has these 10 cards.   He shuffles them and puts them face down.

If you pick a card, what is the probability that you will pick
(a) an ace   (b) a two   (c) a three   (d) a red card

Ordinary dice are made in the shape of a cube.

Imagine a dice like this.

It would not be fair.
If you throw it, it is much more likely to land
this way   than this way.

With an ordinary cubical dice, **all six numbers are equally likely** to come up.

C4 What is the probability of throwing a five with an ordinary dice?

D The Wheel of Fortune

This picture and the picture below show a
'Wheel of Fortune' stall at a fair.

People buy tickets to play. There are
20 tickets, numbered 1 to 20.

When all the tickets are sold, the stall
keeper spins the pointer. When the pointer
stops, the number it points to is the winning
number.

The 20 parts of the circle are all equal, so
the **20 numbers are all equally likely to win**.

D1 You have bought ticket number 6.
What is the probability that the winning number will be 6?

D2 Each ticket costs 10p.

(a) How much money does the stall keeper take when all the
tickets are sold?

(b) The prize for the winner is a ball worth £1·25.
How much profit does the stall keeper make each time the
game is played? (All tickets are sold each time.)

D3 **A question for discussion**
Suppose you buy three tickets. Is it better to have them next to
each other, or spaced out? Or doesn't it matter?

D4 You are running a school fête. Someone has made a Wheel of
Fortune. Before it is used, you want to test it to see if it is fair.
How could you do this?

E Roulette

A roulette wheel is divided into 37 equal parts, numbered 0 to 36.

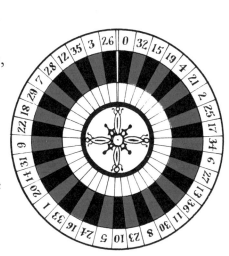

Apart from 0, which is special, half the numbers 1 to 36 are red and half are black.

The wheel is rotated and a little ball is rolled onto it as it goes round. After a while the ball stops against one of the numbers, which is the winning number.

Roulette is played between players and the 'bank'.
The simplest way to play is for a player to bet on either red or black.

Suppose a player bets 10p on red. If the ball lands on a red number, the bank pays him 10p and he gets his own 10p back. If the ball lands on black, he loses his 10p.

If the ball lands on zero, his 10p goes into 'prison'. The wheel is spun again. If the ball lands on red, he gets his own 10p back (but no more). If it lands on black, he loses his 10p.

E1 A person bets 10p on red.

(a) What is the probability that the ball lands on a red number?

(b) What is the probability that the ball lands on a black number (not counting 0)?

(c) What is the probability that the ball lands on 0?

The game is not fair. The bank is in a better position than the player. If the ball lands on 0, the bank has a chance of winning 10p, but the player has no chance of winning 10p. He can only get his own money back.

E2 Another way of playing is to bet on one single number (but not 0). If this number wins, the bank pays 35 times the amount which the player bet.

Suppose there are 36 players and each one bets £1 on a different number.

(a) If the winning number is not 0, but one of the numbers 1 to 36, how much does the bank take, and how much does it pay out?

(b) If the winning number is 0, how much does the bank take?

(c) Is this game fair, or does the bank have an advantage?

F Raffles

Many clubs hold raffles to raise money.
They sell raffle tickets. Each ticket is in two parts,
with the same number on each part.

One part is given to the person who buys the ticket.
The other part goes into a box, to wait for the 'draw'.

When the draw is held, the box of tickets is
shaken up. Someone puts his or her hand into
the box without looking, and takes out a ticket.

The person with that number wins the prize.

Every ticket has the same chance of winning.

F1 A football club holds a Christmas raffle. The prize is a
bottle of sherry. 100 tickets are sold.

(a) Jane has bought one ticket (number 58). What is the probability
that she will win the prize?

(b) Sam has bought three tickets. What is the probability that
he will win the prize?

(c) The tickets cost 10p each. How much money does the club
take altogether from selling tickets?

(d) The bottle of sherry cost the club £2·40. How much profit
will the club make?

(e) If you buy five raffle tickets, is it better to have five numbers
next to each other (for example, 43, 44, 45, 46, 47) or five
numbers spaced out?

F2 Peter and Linda are having an argument. Peter has bought
ticket number 53 and Linda has bought number 1.

Special numbers like 1 or 100 never win. The winner is much more likely to be an ordinary number, like 53.

Don't be silly! Every number has the same chance of winning. So 1 is just as likely to win as 53.

Who do you think is right?

F3 The football club has a raffle for a bottle of sherry every Christmas.

The club chairman suggests a new way of selling tickets.
He suggests that tickets are sold in fives instead of ones.
People would pay 10p for five tickets instead of 10p for one.

The chairman says this will give people a better chance of winning, because each person will have five numbers instead of one.
Is the chairman right?

F4 A youth club organises a raffle to raise money for records.
The prize is a microcomputer which cost £45.
Tickets are 25p each.

(a) How many tickets have to be sold to cover the cost of the prize?

(b) In fact, 500 tickets are sold. How much profit does the club make from the raffle?

(c) Shirley has bought tickets 160, 161, 162, 163 and 164.
What is the probability that she will win the prize?

G Throwing coins and dice: class activities

A fair coin is one which is evenly balanced. When you throw it, 'head' and 'tail' are equally likely.

G1 (Discussion question)
Sandra has thrown an ordinary fair coin five times.
It has landed 'head' five times. Which of these is true for the next throw?

(a) 'Head' is more likely than 'tail'.

(b) 'Tail' is more likely than 'head'.

(c) 'Head' and 'tail' are equally likely.

G2 This is an activity to be done in pairs. Each pair needs two coins.

Ray said: 'When you throw two coins, three things can happen. Either you get two heads, or two tails, or one head and one tail. So the probability of each of these things is $\frac{1}{3}$.'

If Ray is right, then if you throw two coins again and again you should get roughly equal numbers of 'two heads', 'two tails' and 'one head, one tail'.

Throw two coins many times. Keep a tally of the number of times you get 'two heads', 'two tails' and 'one head, one tail'.
Put all the class's results together.

When you throw two coins again and again, you find that 'one head and one tail' comes up more often than either 'two heads' or 'two tails'.

There is a reason for this.

Call the two coins A and B. There are **four** things which can happen when the two coins are thrown.

These four results are all equally likely.

The probability of getting 'two heads' is 1 out of 4, or $\frac{1}{4}$.
The probability of getting 'two tails' is also $\frac{1}{4}$.
The probability of getting 'one head and one tail' is $\frac{2}{4}$ or $\frac{1}{2}$.

When you did your experiment with two coins, you put together the results which were either
A B   A B
(T)(H) or (T)(H) and called them
all 'one head, one tail'.

G3   This is an activity for pairs. Each pair needs two dice.

(a) When you throw two dice, the total score you get can be 2, 3, 4, 5, 6, 7, 8, 9, 10, 11 or 12.

Make a tally like the one below. Throw the two dice many times and fill in the table.

Score		Frequency
2		
3		
4		
(and so on up to)		
12		
	Total	

(b) Collect all the class's results together and draw a frequency stick graph to show them.

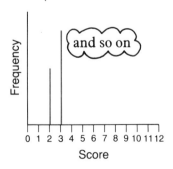

(Continued on next page.)

(c) Which of these frequency graphs do your results look like most?

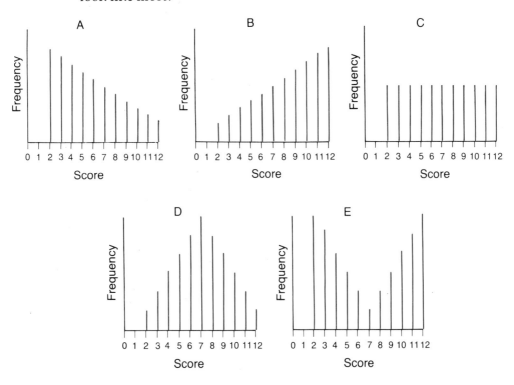

The next question helps to explain why the frequency graph has the shape it has.

G4 This is the start of a table showing all the different ways in which the two dice can fall. (The dice are called A and B.)

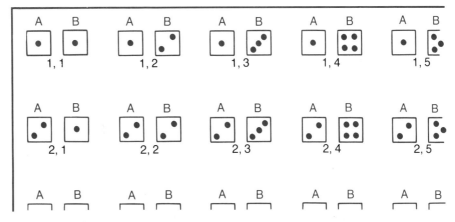

(a) Copy and complete the table. Write down only the number-pairs shown in black. Do not draw all the pictures.

(b) How many different pairs are there?

Look through the table you made for question G4.
Only one pair gives a total score of 2. It is the pair 1, 1.

A   B

There are 36 possible pairs and they are all equally likely.
So the probability of getting a total score of 2 is 1 out of 36, or $\frac{1}{36}$.

G5 (a) How many pairs give a total score of 3?

    (b) What is the probability of getting a total score of 3?

    (c) How many pairs give a total score of 4?

    (d) What is the probability of getting a total score of 4?

G6 What is the probability of getting a total score of

    (a) 5   (b) 6   (c) 7   (d) 8   (e) 9   (f) 10   (g) 11   (h) 12

G7 (a) Which total score is the most likely of all?

    (b) Did this score come up most often in your class experiment?

G8 Suppose you have two dice each in the shape of a **regular octahedron**.
(A regular octahedron has 8 identical faces.)

The faces of each dice are numbered from 1 to 8.

A 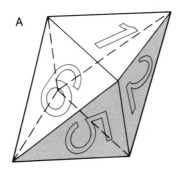 B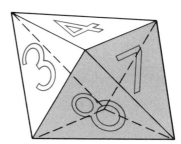

    (a) Call the dice A and B.
    Make a list of all the possible pairs of numbers you can get
    when the two dice are thrown.

    Write each pair like this: 4, 7   This means 4 on A and 7 on B.

    (b) How many different pairs of numbers are there?

    (c) How many pairs give a total score of 10?

    (d) What is the probability of getting a total score of 10?

    (e) Which is the most likely total score? What is the probability
    of getting this score?

H Comparing probabilities

Suppose you are very fond of red sweets, but you hate black ones.

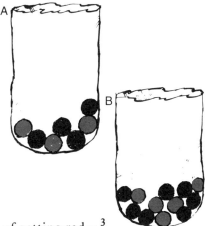

Someone asks you to choose between the two bags A and B shown here. When you have chosen your bag, it is shaken up. You are allowed to take out one sweet without looking.

Obviously you want to choose the bag which gives the highest probability of getting a red sweet. So first you calculate the probability of taking a red sweet from A, and the probability of taking a red sweet from B.

Bag A   3 red sweets out of 7 altogether. Probability of getting red $= \frac{3}{7}$

Bag B   5 red sweets out of 12 altogether. Probability of getting red $= \frac{5}{12}$

Now you need to know which is greater, $\frac{3}{7}$ or $\frac{5}{12}$.

You can find out by changing both fractions to **decimals**, on a calculator.

$\frac{3}{7}$ $3 \div 7$ $= 0.428\ldots$ $\frac{5}{12}$ $5 \div 12$ $= 0.416\ldots$

So $\frac{3}{7}$ is greater than $\frac{5}{12}$.

So **bag A** gives the higher probability of getting a red sweet.

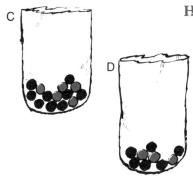

H1 (a) What is the probability of picking out a red sweet from bag C? (Write it as a fraction.)

(b) Change the fraction to a decimal.

(c) What is the probability of picking out a red sweet from bag D? (Write it as a fraction.)

(d) Change the fraction to a decimal.

(e) Which bag gives the higher probability of picking out a red sweet?

H2 Suppose you like black sweets but hate red ones.

Which of the bags E and F gives the higher probability of getting a **black** sweet?

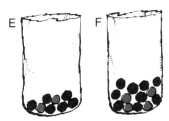

H3 Which of these is more likely: getting a score of six with one throw of a dice, or a total score of six with two throws?
Explain how you get your answer.

6 On paper (1)

Do these calculations on paper (or in your head if you can) **without using a calculator**.

1 (a) $417 + 389$ (b) $618 + 43 + 262$ (c) $2683 + 509$

  (d) £5·86 + £3·05   (e) £12·80 + £7·49   (f) £58·75 + £26

2 (a) $372 - 146$ (b) $509 - 268$ (c) $1382 - 773$

  (d) $1600 - 583$ (e) $670 - 264$ (f) $1005 - 377$

3 (a) 761×5 (b) 423×4 (c) 682×3

  (d) 908×6 (e) 537×10 (f) 7×234

4 (a) $364 \div 4$ (b) $708 \div 3$ (c) $444 \div 6$

  (d) $865 \div 5$ (e) $1608 \div 2$ (f) $2832 \div 4$

5 Four people go on a coach trip. The cost is £3·60 each. How much does that come to altogether?

6 When I came home from shopping I had £4·83 in my bag. When I left home I had £7·50. How much did I spend?

7 A customer bought a camera for £26·95. It was faulty, so the shop agreed to refund the money. The customer decided to buy a different camera, which cost £41·50. How much extra did he have to pay?

8 Six people bought a 'winebox' to take to a party. They agreed to share the cost equally. The winebox cost £8·70. How much did each person pay?

9 Dawn went on a journey for her firm and her firm agreed to pay her expenses. Her train fares came to £16·85 and her meals to £3·48. What was the total of her expenses?

10 Seven people shared out 468 eggs between them. Each person got the same number but some were left over.

How many did each person get, and how many eggs were left over?

Review 1

1 Using a calculator

1.1 Work these out on your calculator.

(a) $(5\cdot6 + 2\cdot9) \times 1\cdot8$ (b) $5\cdot6 + (2\cdot9 \times 1\cdot8)$

(c) $7\cdot3 + (0\cdot8 \times 6\cdot7)$ (d) $(7\cdot3 + 0\cdot8) \times 6\cdot7$

(e) $3\cdot2 \times (7\cdot1 - 5\cdot3)$ (f) $(3\cdot2 \times 7\cdot1) - 5\cdot3$

1.2 Use your calculator to work out the value of $a + bc$ when a is 136, b is 43 and c is 17.

1.3 Work these out on your calculator. Give each answer to 2 d.p.

(a) $\dfrac{36\cdot2}{1\cdot7} + 8\cdot5$ (b) $\dfrac{4\cdot3 + 10\cdot9}{3\cdot5}$ (c) $16\cdot4 + \dfrac{28\cdot3}{5\cdot4}$

(d) $\dfrac{17\cdot6 - 13\cdot8}{4\cdot7}$ (e) $13\cdot7 + \dfrac{1\cdot9}{0\cdot3}$ (f) $2\cdot8 + \dfrac{6\cdot8}{1\cdot4}$

2 In your head (1)

Do these in your head as quickly as you can.

2.1 (a) 4×9 (b) 5×7 (c) $28 \div 4$ (d) $36 \div 6$ (e) $32 \div 4$

2.2 (a) $27 + 13$ (b) $58 + 14$ (c) $63 - 22$ (d) $53 - 28$ (e) $44 - 17$

2.3 Write each of these fractions as a decimal.

(a) $\frac{9}{10}$ (b) $\frac{49}{100}$ (c) $\frac{4}{5}$ (d) $\frac{3}{4}$ (e) $\frac{3}{100}$

2.4 A TV programme starts at 9:15 and finishes at 9:50. How long does it last?

2.5 Multiply each of these numbers by 10.

(a) $6\cdot8$ (b) 41 (c) $0\cdot08$ (d) $4\cdot36$ (e) $12\cdot04$

2.6 Change these measurements to centimetres.

(a) $4\,\text{m}$ (b) $3\cdot6\,\text{m}$ (c) $0\cdot2\,\text{m}$ (d) $0\cdot54\,\text{m}$ (e) $13\cdot5\,\text{m}$

2.7 I bought 3 metres of ribbon. I used 45 cm of it on a dress. How much did I have left?

3 Views

3.1 A paper cup, a yogurt pot and a tin are standing on a table.

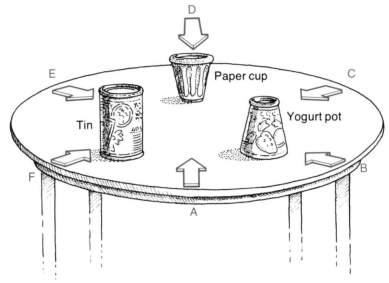

When you look in the direction of arrow A, you see this view:

(a) In which direction do you look to see each of these views?

(i) ▽△□   (ii) △□▽

(b) Draw the view looking in the direction of   (i) arrow F   (ii) arrow D

4 Time

4.1 Shadrach went for an interview. It lasted from 9:25 a.m. to 11:10 a.m.
How long did the interview last?

4.2 How long is it   (a) from 04:45 to 08:20   (b) from 07:50 to 09:05
(c) from 12:10 to 15:45   (d) from 06:35 to 09:25

4.3 A film which lasts for 3 hours 40 minutes starts at 6:45 p.m.
When does it end?

4.4 A club is organising a coach outing to Brighton. They are told
it will take $3\frac{3}{4}$ hours to get there. The coach leaves at 07:20.
When will it get to Brighton?

34

5 Probability

5.1 Linda has 12 cards with numbers on them. Here they are:

$$\boxed{1}\ \boxed{1}\ \boxed{1}\ \boxed{2}\ \boxed{2}\ \boxed{3}\ \boxed{4}\ \boxed{5}\ \boxed{6}\ \boxed{7}\ \boxed{8}\ \boxed{9}$$

She shuffles the cards and puts them face down.

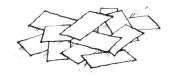

Her friend Kate takes a card.
What is the probability that the number
on Kate's card is

(a) 1   (b) 2   (c) 3   (d) greater than 3   (e) even   (f) odd

(g) divisible by 3   (h) divisible by 4   (i) a factor of 12

5.2 A box of coloured sweets contains
    4 red   3 green   5 brown   6 yellow   2 orange

(a) Hitesh's favourite colour is red. If he shakes the box and takes
out a sweet without looking, what is the probability that he
will take out a red sweet?

(b) Hitesh hates yellow sweets and orange sweets. What is the probability
that he will get a colour he hates?

(c) Hitesh shakes the box and takes out a sweet. It is red. He eats it.
He shakes the box again. If he takes out another sweet, what is the
probability that it will be red?

5.3 Hitesh's favourite colour is red.
If he had to pick a sweet from
one of these bags without looking,
which bag should he choose?

Explain how you get your answer.

A    B

6 On paper (1)

Do these without using a calculator.

6.1 (a) $1408 + 736$ (b) $1203 - 586$ (c) $1600 - 247$

6.2 (a) 183×4 (b) $624 \div 3$ (c) $2508 \div 6$

6.3 A milkman left the dairy with 854 pints of milk, and returned
with 167 pints. How many pints did he deliver?

6.4 Seven people share out some money equally. Each one gets £3·75.
How much money was shared out?

7 Multiplication patterns

Everyone (or nearly everyone) knows that $3 \times 4 = 12$.
Starting from 3×4 you can get many other multiplications.

For example, if you change the 3 to 30 (by multiplying by 10), you get
$30 \times 4 = 120$. Notice that the answer is also 10 times what it was before.

$$3 \quad \times \quad 4 \qquad\qquad 12$$
multiply by 10 → 30
multiply by 10 → 120
$$30 \quad \times \quad 4 \quad = \quad 120$$

Now if we multiply the 4 by 10 as well, the answer is multiplied by 10 again.

$$30 \quad \times \quad 4 \quad = \quad 120$$
multiply by 10 → 40
multiply by 10 → 1200
$$30 \quad \times \quad 40 \quad = \quad 1200$$

Now suppose we multiply the 40 by 10. The answer is multiplied by 10 again.

$$30 \quad \times \quad 40 \quad = \quad 1200$$
multiply by 10 → 400
multiply by 10 → 12000
$$30 \quad \times \quad 400 \quad = \quad 12\,000$$

And so we can go on.

1 Start with $5 \times 3 = 15$

   Write down some other multiplications you can get from this one, by multiplying the numbers by 10.

2 Start with $3 \times 2 = 6$, and work out

   (a) 30×2 (b) 30×20 (c) 300×20 (d) 300×200

3 Work out   (a) 40×50 (b) 600×30 (c) 400×200 (d) 7000×30

Suppose we start again with $3 \times 4 = 12$.
If you change 3 to 0·3 (by dividing by 10) you get $0·3 \times 4 = 1·2$.
Notice that the answer has also been divided by 10.

$$3 \quad \times \quad 4 \quad = \quad 12$$

divide by 10   divide by 10

$$0·3 \quad \times \quad 4 \quad = \quad 1·2$$

Now if we divide the 4 by 10 as well, the answer is divided by 10 again.

$$0·3 \quad \times \quad 4 \quad = \quad 1·2$$

divide by 10   divide by 10

$$0·3 \quad \times \quad 0·4 \quad = \quad 0·12$$

And so we can go on.

4   Start with $5 \times 3 = 15$, and work out   (a) $5 \times 0·3$ (b) $0·5 \times 0·3$

5   Start with $3 \times 2 = 6$, and work out   (a) $0·3 \times 2$ (b) $0·3 \times 0·2$

6   Work out   (a) $0·5 \times 8$ (b) $0·6 \times 0·2$ (c) $0·3 \times 0·3$

Now we will see what happens when we sometimes multiply by 10 and sometimes divide by 10. We start with $3 \times 4 = 12$ again.

Each black arrow means 'multiply by 10'.
Each red arrow means 'divide by 10'.

$$3 \quad \times \quad 4 \quad = \quad 12$$
$$3 \quad \times \quad 40 \quad = \quad 120$$
$$0·3 \quad \times \quad 40 \quad = \quad 12$$
$$0·03 \quad \times \quad 40 \quad = \quad 1·2$$

7   Start with $3 \times 5 = 15$, and work out
     (a) $0·3 \times 5$ (b) $0·3 \times 50$ (c) $0·3 \times 500$

Worked example

Work out 0.04×50 without using a calculator.

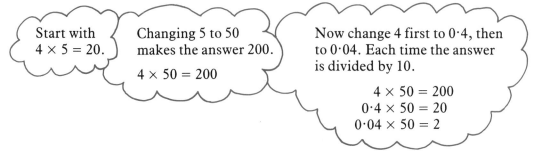

Start with
$4 \times 5 = 20$.

Changing 5 to 50
makes the answer 200.

$4 \times 50 = 200$

Now change 4 first to 0.4, then
to 0.04. Each time the answer
is divided by 10.

$4 \times 50 = 200$
$0.4 \times 50 = 20$
$0.04 \times 50 = 2$

After some practice you will be able to do most of it in your head.

Answer the questions below **without using a calculator**.

8   Start with $3 \times 6 = 18$ and work out

    (a) 3×60 (b) 3×600 (c) 0.3×600

9   Start with $5 \times 8 = 40$ and work out

    (a) 50×8 (b) 50×0.8 (c) 50×0.08

10   Start with $7 \times 3 = 21$ and work out

    (a) 7×30 (b) 7×300 (c) 0.7×300 (d) 0.07×300

11   Work out 40×0.06.

12   Work out 0.02×700.

13   Work out 5000×0.3.

14   Work out 400×0.05.

15   After a disaster a government decides to give people emergency
rations. Each person will get

       0.4 kilogram rice
       0.3 litre milk
       20 gram salt

An emergency centre is set up to provide rations for 600 people.

    (a) Work out the total amount of rice needed for 600 people.

    (b) Work out the total amount of milk needed.

    (c) Work out the total amount of salt needed, in grams.

8 Enlargement and reduction (1)

A Enlargements on squared paper

Picture B is a **2 times enlargement** of picture A.

Every line in picture B is 2 times as long as in picture A.

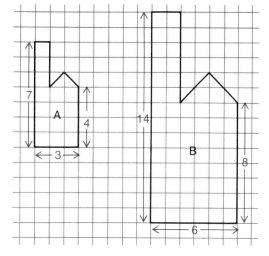

A1 In the diagram below, an artist is making a 2 times enlargement of a shape.

So far it has been easy, because all the lines have been either across the page or up the page.

How should the artist draw the next line, which slopes downwards?

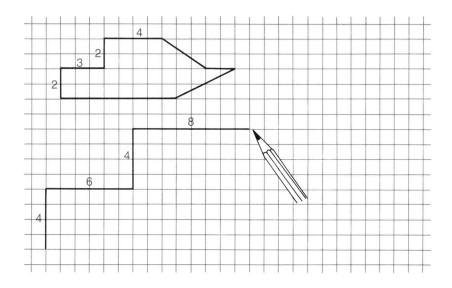

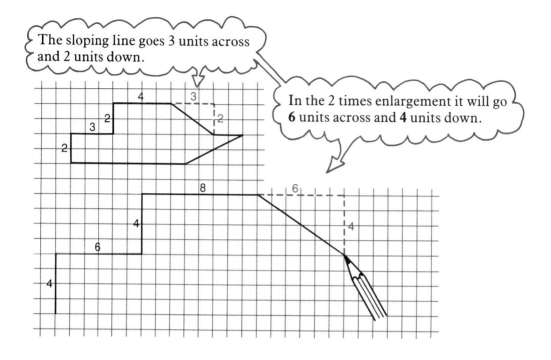

The sloping line goes 3 units across and 2 units down.

In the 2 times enlargement it will go **6** units across and **4** units down.

A2 *You need worksheet B4–2.*

(a) Complete the 2 times enlargement on the worksheet.

(b) Make 2 times enlargements of each of the other shapes on the worksheet.

Shape D is a 3 times enlargement of shape C.

Every line in D is 3 times as long as in C.

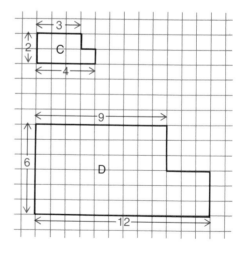

A3 *You need worksheet B4–3.*

(a) Make a 3 times enlargement of the first shape on the worksheet.

(b) Make a $1\frac{1}{2}$ times enlargement of the second shape.

B The scale factor of an enlargement

Look again at shapes C and D in the lower diagram on the opposite page.

Shape D is a 3 times enlargement of shape C. We say the **scale factor** of the enlargement is 3.

> **B1** Look at shapes C and D again.
> Suppose you had not been told that the scale factor of the enlargement is 3.
> How could you work out the scale factor from the measurements marked on the drawings?
>
> **B2** Shape E is enlarged to make shape F.
> Work out the scale factor of the enlargement and explain how you did it.

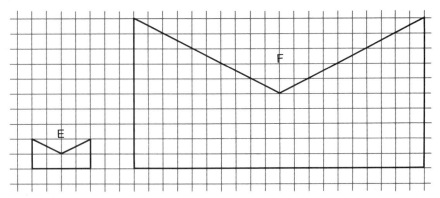

> **B3** In this example the numbers are not so 'easy'.
> What calculation would you do on a calculator to work out the scale factor of the enlargement?
>
> (For example, would you do 18 + 126?)

18 mm

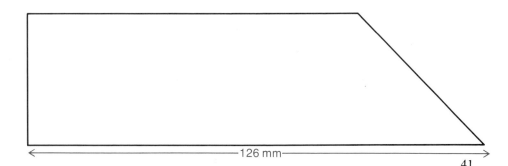

126 mm

41

You can calculate the scale factor of an enlargement like this.

1 Choose a length in the original picture and see what it is enlarged to.

   Here 1·8 cm has been enlarged to 4·5 cm.

2 Divide the new length by the original length.

   Scale factor $= \dfrac{\text{New length}}{\text{Original length}}$

   $\qquad\quad = \dfrac{4·5}{1·8} = 2·5$

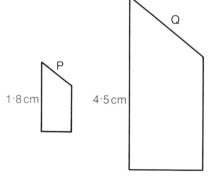

B4 Calculate the scale factor of each of these enlargements. Round off to 1 decimal place where necessary.

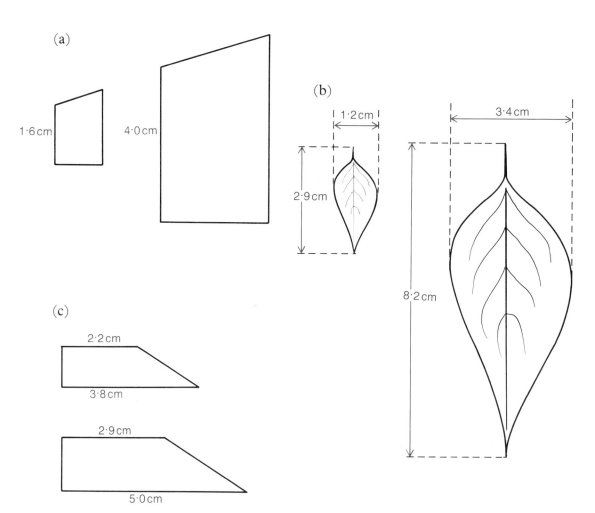

(a)

1·6 cm   4·0 cm

(b)

1·2 cm   3·4 cm

2·9 cm   8·2 cm

(c)

2·2 cm
3·8 cm

2·9 cm
5·0 cm

C Reduction

Picture A has been **reduced** to make picture B.

Every length in B is $\frac{1}{2}$ of what it is in A.

We call this a $\frac{1}{2}$ **times reduction**.

The scale factor of this reduction is $\frac{1}{2}$, or 0·5.

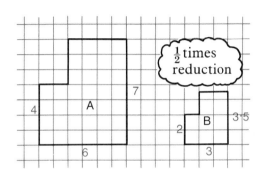

(A reduction is the 'opposite' of an enlargement.
B is a $\frac{1}{2}$ times reduction of A, but A is also a 2 times enlargement of B.)

You need worksheet B4–4 for questions C1 and C2.

C1 Make a $\frac{1}{2}$ times reduction of each shape.

C2 Make a $\frac{1}{3}$ times reduction of each shape.
(Every length in the reduction is $\frac{1}{3}$ of the original length.)

C3 Find the scale factor of each of these reductions.
Each scale factor is a simple fraction.

(a)

(b)

(c)

(d)

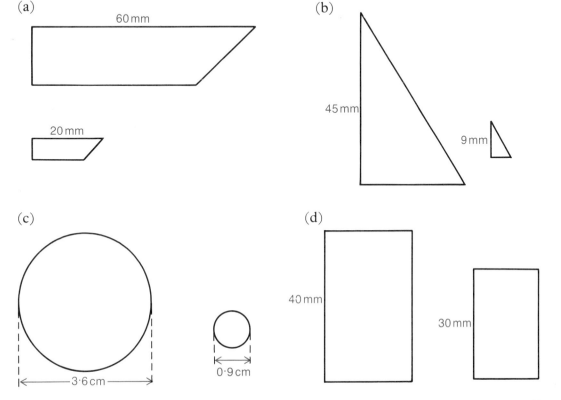

43

9 Percentage

A Calculating a percentage of a quantity

Sharon is painting a fence.

Here is the fence divided up into 100 equal parts.
Sharon has painted 85 out of the 100 parts.
So she has painted **85%** of the fence.

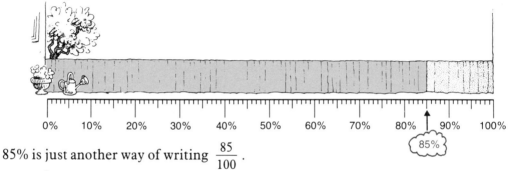

85% is just another way of writing $\dfrac{85}{100}$.

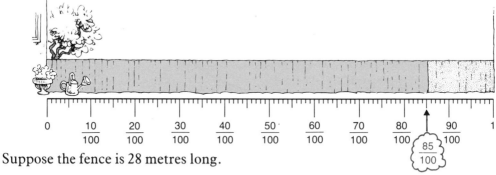

Suppose the fence is 28 metres long.

Sharon has painted **85% of 28 metres**.

This means the same as $\dfrac{85}{100}$ of 28 metres.

To do it on a calculator we have to remember that $\dfrac{85}{100}$ can be

written as a decimal. It is $0\cdot85$.

To work out $\dfrac{85}{100}$ of 28 metres we do **$0\cdot85 \times 28$**.

It comes to $23\cdot8$ metres.

Remember . . .

$$\text{Percentage} \qquad \text{Fraction} \qquad \text{Decimal}$$

$$85\% \qquad = \qquad \frac{85}{100} \qquad = \qquad 0{\cdot}85$$

Worked example

Work out 36% of £170.

Think: $36\% = \dfrac{36}{100} = \mathbf{0{\cdot}36.}$ **Do:** $0{\cdot}36 \times 170 = 61{\cdot}2$

Answer **£61·20.**

A1 (a) Copy and complete: $44\% = \dfrac{\cdots}{100} = 0{\cdot}\ldots$

     (b) Use a calculator to work out 44% of 28 metres.

A2 (a) Copy and complete: $73\% = \dfrac{\cdots}{100} = 0{\cdot}\ldots$

     (b) Use a calculator to work out 73% of £520.

A3 Work out

     (a) 35% of £650   (b) 26% of £132   (c) 70% of £86

Tricky ones

8% as a fraction is $\dfrac{8}{100}$. As a decimal, this is $0{\cdot}08$ (**not** $0{\cdot}8$).

$$\text{Percentage} \qquad \text{Fraction} \qquad \text{Decimal}$$

$$8\% \qquad = \qquad \frac{8}{100} \qquad = \qquad 0{\cdot}08$$

A4 (a) Copy and complete: $3\% = \dfrac{\cdots}{100} = 0{\cdot}\ldots$

     (b) Work out 3% of 28 metres.

A5 Work out

     (a) 4% of £180   (b) 7% of £96   (c) 9% of £280

A6 Sarah gets a pay rise of 8%. Before, she was paid £563 a month.

     (a) Calculate 8% of £563.

     (b) Calculate Sarah's new monthly pay, after the rise.

B Expressing one quantity as a percentage of another

Worked example

A fire destroyed 29 km² of forest, out of a total area of 74 km².

What percentage of the forest was destroyed by the fire?

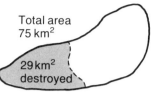

Total area
75 km²

29 km²
destroyed

29 km² out of 74 km² were destroyed.

Write this as a fraction: $\frac{29}{74}$ of the forest was destroyed.

Change the fraction to a decimal, by dividing 'top' by 'bottom'.

$\frac{29}{74} = 29 \div 74 = 0\cdot391\,89\ldots$

Round off to 2 decimal places: $0\cdot39$.

Now change $0\cdot39$ to a percentage.

$0\cdot39 = \frac{39}{100} = \textbf{39\%}$.

B1 A gardener planted 45 shrubs. 17 of them were killed by frost. What percentage of the shrubs were killed by frost?

B2 A zoo has 26 male tortoises and 35 female tortoises. What percentage of the tortoises are male?

(If you get the answer 74%, think again!)

B3 A company has 405 employees. 327 of them are on strike. What percentage of the employees are still at work?

B4 This table gives information about the weekly earnings of the employees of another company.

Weekly earnings	Number of employees
less than £100	26
£100–£199	174
£200–£299	106
£300 or over	39

(a) How many employees are there altogether?

(b) What percentage of them earn   (i) less than £100   (ii) £200 or more

C Mixed questions

C1 A large farm has a total area of $4 \cdot 8 \, \text{km}^2$.
$3 \cdot 1 \, \text{km}^2$ of the farm is used for growing wheat.

What percentage of the farm is used for growing wheat?

C2 A school fair raises £682 for charity. It is agreed to
divide the money between three charities, like this:

65% to Save the Children   20% to Help the Aged   15% to Cancer Research

How much money does each charity get?

C3 (a) **Estimate** what percentage of this strip is coloured red.
Write down your estimate.

(b) Now measure the total length of the strip, and the length
of the coloured part.
From your measurements calculate what percentage of the
strip is coloured.
Compare the result with your estimate.

C4 Repeat question C3 for this strip.

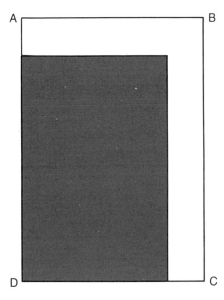

C5 (a) Estimate what percentage of the area
of the rectangle ABCD is coloured.
Write down your estimate.

(b) Measure the sides of ABCD, and
of the coloured rectangle.
Calculate their areas.

(c) Calculate the percentage of the
area of ABCD which is coloured.
Was your estimate too high or
too low?

10 Approximation

A Rounding off: a reminder

A reference book gives the population of Penzance as 19 427.
It is not usually necessary to know the size of the population as exactly
as this. A rough idea, or **approximation**, is good enough. (In any case
the population is always changing, as people are born, die or move around.)

You can round off the population to the **nearest thousand**.
19 427 is between 19 thousand and 20 thousand, but it is
closer to 19 000 than to 20 000.
So when you round off 19 427 to the nearest thousand, you get **19 000**.

If you round off 26 524 to the nearest thousand, you get **27 000**.
This is because 26 524 is closer to 27 000 than to 26 000.
You can see this by looking at the hundreds figure. If it is 5 or more,
then you round **up**.

A1 Round off each of these populations to the nearest thousand.

(a) Gloucester 90 246   (b) Dover 34 429   (c) Inverness 34 839

(d) Cardiff 279 142   (e) Blackpool 151 927   (f) Harrogate 62 513

A2 Round off each of these numbers to the nearest **hundred**.

(a) 623   (b) 871   (c) 1244   (d) 3487   (e) 8885

(f) 4082   (g) 16 734   (h) 35 871   (i) 12 986   (j) 850 066

A3 Round off each of these numbers to 1 decimal place.

(a) 0·872   (b) 0·316   (c) 0·5984   (d) 7·362   (e) 5·083

(f) 7·775   (g) 1·058   (h) 92·383   (i) 48·067   (j) 51·349

A4 Round off

(a) 6·2732 to 2 d.p.   (b) 69 287 to the nearest hundred

(c) 45 267 to the nearest hundred   (d) 0·083 62 to 1 d.p.

(e) 5·680 km to the nearest 0·1 km   (f) 5·8967 to 2 d.p.

A5 Do each of these on a calculator, and round off the answer
to 2 decimal places.

(a) 7·38 × 0·56   (b) 14·92 × 8·61   (c) 12·03 × 0·084

(d) 51·36 ÷ 24·9   (e) 0·872 ÷ 0·17   (f) 15·63 ÷ 0·007

B Rough estimates

Charlie is a gardener. He wants to know **roughly** the area of this rectangular lawn.

He has no calculator, so he will have to work out a rough answer in his head.

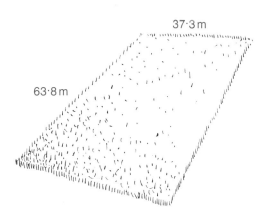

37·3 m

63·8 m

What is 63·8 × 37·3 roughly?

His friend Heather has an idea.

Why don't you round off the length and width to the nearest whole number?
You can do 64 × 37 to get a rough answer.

But that's still too hard.
I can't do 64 × 37 without a calculator.

Charlie himself has a better idea.

I'll round off the length and width to the nearest ten.
63·8 is roughly **60**.
37·3 is roughly **40**.

I can do 60 × 40 in my head.
60 × 40 = **2400**.
So the area is roughly 2400 m².

Charlie's method gives only a rough answer for the area of the lawn.
But it may be good enough. (The 'exact' answer is 2379·74 m².)

Many people need to work out rough answers, or **rough estimates**.
They round off the numbers until they get a calculation they can do easily.

B1 Work out a rough answer in your head for each of these.

(a) 41·2 × 28·7   (b) 68·9 × 32·1   (c) 51·3 × 32·5

(d) 78·3 × 20·8   (e) 19·6 × 18·9   (f) 88·7 × 38·2

B2 Explain how you get a rough answer in your head for this calculation: 213 × 4·86

49

There are several ways to get a rough answer for 213×4.86.
Here is the simplest way:

Round off 213 to the nearest hundred. 213 becomes 200.

Round off 4·86 to the nearest whole number. 4·86 becomes 5.

So do $200 \times 5 = \mathbf{1000}$.

B3 Work out a rough estimate for 78.5×5.93.

(Round off 78·5 to the nearest ten, and 5·93 to the nearest whole number.)

B4 Work out a rough estimate for 51.8×0.687.

(Round off 51·8 to the nearest ten, and 0·687 to the nearest tenth, or 1 decimal place.)

B5 (a) Without using a calculator, estimate roughly the cost of 18·6 m of material at £6·85 a metre.

(b) Use a calculator to work out the exact cost.

B6 (a) A train consists of 48 trucks. If each truck can hold 38·5 tonnes, estimate roughly the total weight the train can carry.

(b) Use a calculator to calculate the total weight.

B7 (a) A concert hall has room for 826 people. If each person pays £2·90 for a ticket, estimate roughly how much money a full house will bring in.

(b) Use a calculator to find the exact amount.

B8 Without using a calculator, work out a rough estimate for each of these.

(a) 22.4×307.9 (b) 0.421×88.9 (c) 716.3×0.288

(d) 47.6×49.3 (e) 308.5×7.82 (f) 0.392×0.587

(g) 0.679×315.6 (h) 0.184×41.6 (i) 80.7×493.6

Now use a calculator and see how close you got to each exact answer.

B9 (a) Without using a calculator, estimate the area of the playground shown here.

(b) Use a calculator to find the area.

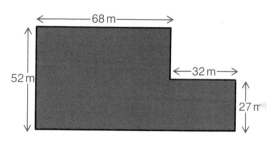

50

These plans show the ground floor and the first floor of a new house. The scale is **1 cm to 1 m**.

B10 (a) Measure the plan to find the length and width of the back room in m.
    (b) Work out in your head a rough value for the area of that room in m².
    (c) The owners of the new house have chosen the kind of carpet they want in the back room. It costs £7·99 a square metre.
       Work out in your head roughly what it will cost to carpet that room.

B11 Work out roughly what it will cost to carpet these rooms.
    (a) The front room, at £6·99 a square metre
    (b) The 1st bedroom, at £5·20 a square metre
    (c) The 2nd bedroom, at £4·95 a square metre
    (d) The 3rd bedroom, at £2·90 a square metre

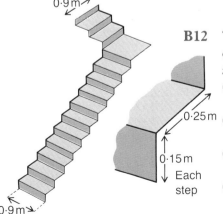

B12 The hall, landing and stairs are all going to be carpeted with the same kind of carpet, costing £9·95 a square metre.
    (a) Find the area of the hall, roughly.
       (It is shaded on the ground floor plan.)
    (b) Find the area of the landing roughly.
       (It is shaded on the first floor plan.)
    (c) The diagram on the left shows the stair carpet. Find its area roughly.
    (d) Work out roughly the total cost of carpeting the hall, stairs and landing.

51

11 Enlargement and reduction (2)

A Enlargements of photographs

Photo A has been **enlarged** to make photo B.

Photo B is 3 times as long as A.
It is also 3 times as high.

3 is the **scale factor** of the enlargement.

A ← 4 cm →
2 cm

B ← 12 cm →
6 cm

A1 (a) Measure the distance between the tops of the two towers on photo A.

(b) Measure the distance in photo B. Check that it is 3 times the distance in A.

A2 Measure the distance between two opposite corners of photo A.
Do the same for photo B and check that the distance in B is 3 times the distance in A.

A3 Suppose you have a lot of copies of photo A (all the same size as A).
How many of them would you need to cover photo B completely?

A4 Imagine an enlargement of A with a scale factor of 4.

(a) What would the dimensions of the enlargement be?

(b) How many copies of photo A would be needed to cover it?

If you did not know the scale factor of the enlargement from photo A to photo B, you could work it out from the measurements.

If you divide the length of B by the length of A, you get the scale factor.

$$\frac{12}{4} = 3$$

You could also get it by dividing the height of B by the height of A.

A5 (a) Measure the heights of photos C and D.

(b) Use your measurements to calculate the scale factor of the enlargement from C to D.

(c) Measure the widths of C and D.

(d) Calculate the scale factor again, using the widths.

A6 Calculate the scale factor of each of these enlargements.

(a)

(b)

The picture frame puzzle

Could you enlarge this photo

to fit this frame exactly?

A7 Solve the puzzle like this:

(a) Measure the length of the photo and the length of the frame. Use these measurements to work out a scale factor.

(b) Now measure the heights of the photo and frame, and use these to work out a scale factor.

If these two 'scale factors' are different, then you cannot enlarge the photo to fit the frame. (You could get the length right but not the height, or the height right but not the length.)

(c) Can the photo be enlarged to fit the frame?

A8 Can this photo be enlarged to fit the frame above?

Explain how you get your answer.

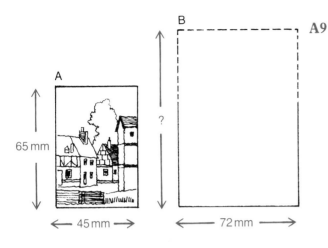

A9 Picture A is to be enlarged to fit the frame B. The problem is to work out the height of B.

(a) Use the widths of A and B to calculate the scale factor of the enlargement.

(b) Multiply the height of A by the scale factor to find the height of B.

A10 Picture C is to be enlarged to fit the frame D.

Calculate

(a) the scale factor of the enlargement

(b) the width of D.

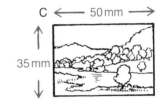

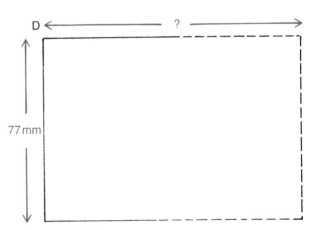

A11 A photo is 80 mm wide and 105 mm high.
It is to be enlarged so that the enlargement is 280 mm wide.

(a) Calculate the scale factor of the enlargement.

(b) Calculate the height of the enlarged photo.

A12 A rare foreign stamp is 3·2 cm by 2·4 cm.
An artist wants to put an enlargement of the stamp on to a poster to advertise an exhibition.

If the longer side of the enlargement is 28 cm, what is the length of the shorter side?

B Practical methods of enlarging

(1) The grid method
One way to enlarge a diagram, such as a map, is to start by drawing a grid on it.

(If you do not want to draw on the map itself, you can use tracing paper.)

You then draw an enlarged grid and copy the map on to it square by square.

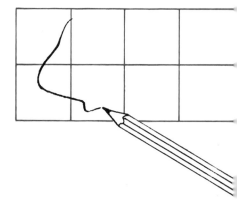

(2) The sloping line method
This is a method for enlarging the 'frame' of a rectangular picture.

Put the picture in the corner of a sheet of paper. Mark a dot at the top corner.

Take the picture away. Draw a sloping line from the bottom corner through the dot.

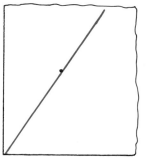

Any rectangle drawn like this will be an enlargement of the frame of the picture.

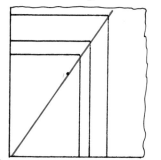

(3) The 'Union Jack' method
You can use this method to enlarge a picture when you have already drawn the enlarged frame by the sloping line method.

Draw these lines on the picture.

Do the same inside the enlarged frame.

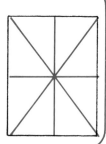

Copy the picture triangle by triangle.

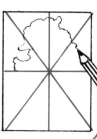

B1 Trace the **frame** of this picture.

(a) Put your tracing in the corner of a piece of paper. Use the sloping line method to enlarge the frame.

(b) Use the 'Union Jack' method to draw an enlargement of the outline of the fish.

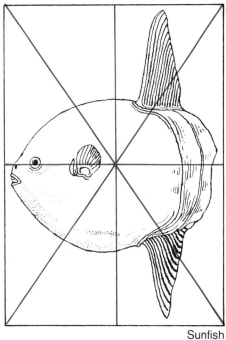

Sunfish

B2 (a) Measure the length and height of the frame of the picture below.

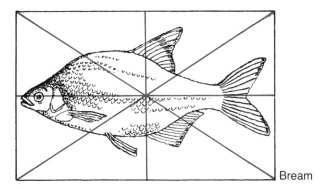

Bream

(b) If the picture is enlarged with a scale factor of 1·2, calculate the length and height of the enlarged frame.

(c) Draw the enlarged frame full-size.
Draw the 'Union Jack' lines on the enlarged frame.
Draw the enlarged outline of the fish.

B3 (a) Can the picture of the sunfish be enlarged to fit a frame which is 153 cm high and 108 cm wide? Explain.

(b) Can the picture of the bream be enlarged to fit a frame which is 168 cm long and 115 cm high? Explain.

57

(4) The 'spider web' method

This method can be used to enlarge a simple diagram, such as a map.
You need to know the scale factor of the enlargement you want.

This is how you use the 'spider web' method to enlarge the outline of a
map, using a scale factor of **1·5**.

1 Mark a point O inside the map.
O is called the **centre of enlargement**.
Draw lines outward from O.

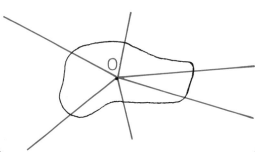

2 Measure the distance from O to each
point where the line crosses the
outline of the map.

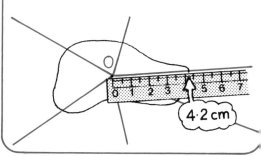

4·2 cm

3 Multiply the distance by the scale
factor, 1·5. Measure the new distance
outwards from O. Mark a new point.

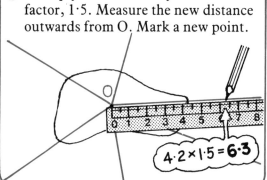

4·2 × 1·5 = **6·3**

4 Do the same on each of the lines.
Join up to get the enlarged map.

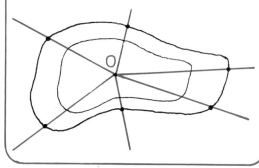

B4 *You need worksheet B4–5.*

Use the 'spider web' method to enlarge each shape on
the worksheet, using the scale factor given.

If the shape has corners, then
make your lines go through
the corners, like this.

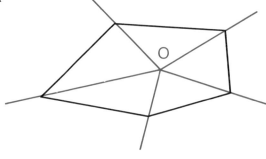

c Reduction

When the scale factor is **less than 1**, we get a **reduction**.
Picture B is a reduction of picture A. The scale factor is 0·6.

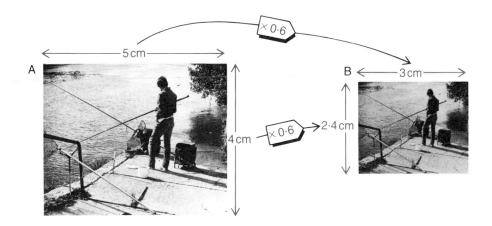

C1 (a) Measure the distance between opposite corners in picture A.

(b) Do the same in picture B.

(c) Check that the distance in B is 0·6 times the distance in A.

If you did not know the scale factor, you could work it out from the
measurements.

1 Choose a length in A and see what it is reduced to.
   For example, 5 cm is reduced to 3 cm.

2 Divide the new length by the original length: $\frac{3}{5}$ = **0·6**.

C2 Calculate the scale factor of this reduction

(a) by measuring the longer sides   (b) by measuring the shorter sides

(c) by measuring across from corner to corner

C3 Calculate the scale factor of each of these reductions.
Give the answer to 2 d.p.

(a)

(b)

(c)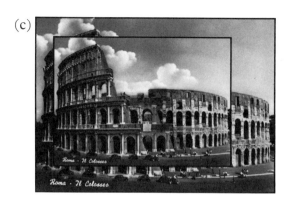

(d)

C4 Picture A is to be reduced to fit the frame B.

A

5·3 cm

6·2 cm

B

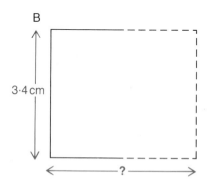

3·4 cm

?

(a) Use the shorter sides of the picture and the frame to calculate the scale factor of the reduction.

(b) Calculate the longer side of the reduced frame.

C5 This model of the Post Office tower is at Tucktonia in Dorset.

(a) Estimate the height of the model tower in metres.

(b) The real tower's height is 190 metres. Estimate the scale factor of the reduction.

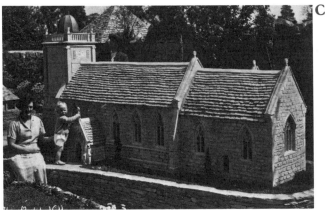

C6 The model village in Bourton-on-the-Water in Gloucestershire is a model of Bourton itself.

The scale factor of the reduction is $\frac{1}{9}$.

(a) Estimate the height of the tower of the model church.

(b) Use your estimate to estimate the height of the tower of the real church.

*C7 The model village in Bourton is a model of Bourton itself. So in the model village there is a model of the model village!

Estimate the height of the tower of the church in the model of the model village.

Review 2

7 Multiplication patterns

7.1 Without using a calculator, work out

(a) 40×50 (b) 300×70 (c) 200×200 (d) 90×8000

7.2 Without using a calculator, work out

(a) $0{\cdot}5 \times 0{\cdot}7$ (b) $0{\cdot}5 \times 0{\cdot}2$ (c) $0{\cdot}03 \times 0{\cdot}8$ (d) $0{\cdot}2 \times 0{\cdot}2$

7.3 Do these without using a calculator.

(a) $30 \times 0{\cdot}5$ (b) $0{\cdot}07 \times 60$ (c) $0{\cdot}02 \times 300$ (d) $200 \times 0{\cdot}01$

8 Enlargement and reduction (1)

8.1 Calculate the scale factor of each of these enlargements.

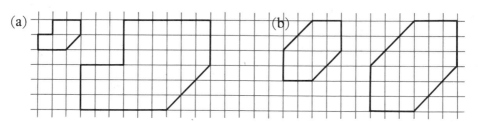

8.2 Calculate the scale factor of each of these enlargements.

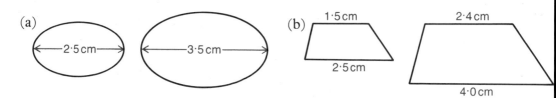

8.3 Calculate the scale factor of each of these **reductions**.

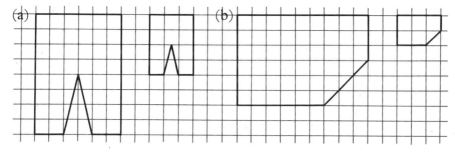

9 Percentage

9.1 Calculate

(a) 35% of £80   (b) 46% of £190   (c) 28% of £73

9.2 Calculate

(a) 8% of £62   (b) 7% of £19   (c) 3% of £265

9.3 There are 782 pupils in a school.
On a particular day, 107 are absent.

What percentage of the pupils are absent?

9.4 Baljit was given £2·50 pocket money.
He spent £1·85 and saved the rest.

What percentage of his pocket money did he save?

9.5 A housing estate has 26 three-bedroomed houses and 10 four-bedroomed houses.

What percentage of the houses are three-bedroomed?

9.6 This table gives information about the ages of the children in a school.

Age in years	5	6	7	8	9
Number of children	23	28	32	31	37

(a) How many children are there in the school?

(b) Calculate what percentage of the children are aged 5.

(c) Calculate the percentage aged 7 or over.

10 Approximation

10.1 Round off

(a) 47 200 to the nearest thousand   (b) 4·684 to 1 decimal place

(c) 583 292 to the nearest hundred   (d) 0·085 61 to 2 d.p.

(e) 6·831 kg to the nearest 0·1 kg   (f) 6·984 to 1 d.p.

10.2 Get a rough answer for each of these, by rounding off the numbers.

(a) 42·6 × 7·93   (b) 61·4 × 39·37   (c) 3·88 × 58·64

(d) 0·37 × 5·24   (e) 48·38 × 0·214   (f) 0·68 × 0·88

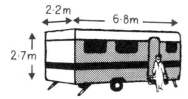

10.3 (a) Without using a calculator, find a rough value for the volume of this caravan, in m³.

(b) Work out the volume on a calculator. Round it off to 1 d.p.

11 Enlargement and reduction (2)

11.1 Picture A has been enlarged to make picture B.

Calculate the scale factor of the enlargement in three ways:

(a) by measuring the longer side of A and B

(b) by measuring the shorter sides of A and B

(c) by measuring the distance across from corner to corner in A and B

11.2 Explain how you can tell that picture C cannot be enlarged to fit the frame D exactly.

11.3 Picture E is to be enlarged to fit the frame F.
Calculate the height of F, showing how you do it.

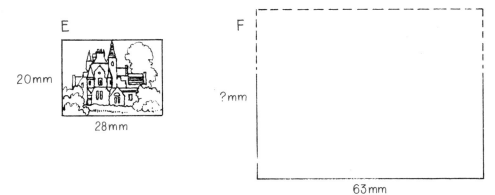

E

20mm

28mm

F

?mm

63mm

11.4 Picture G has been reduced to make picture H.

Measure the pictures and calculate the scale factor of the reduction, to 2 d.p.

G

H

(**Do not write on the book.**)

Clues

Across

3. Three-sided shape.

6. 3 across with all sides equal.

7. 1 down with both pairs of opposite sides equal.

8. 3 across with two sides equal.

Down

1. Four-sided shape.

2. 1 down with all angles equal.

4. 1 down with all angles equal and all sides equal.

5. 1 down with all sides equal.

12 Solids

A Prisms

At a timber yard you can buy lengths of wood with various **cross-sections**.

Here are some of the cross-sections you can get.

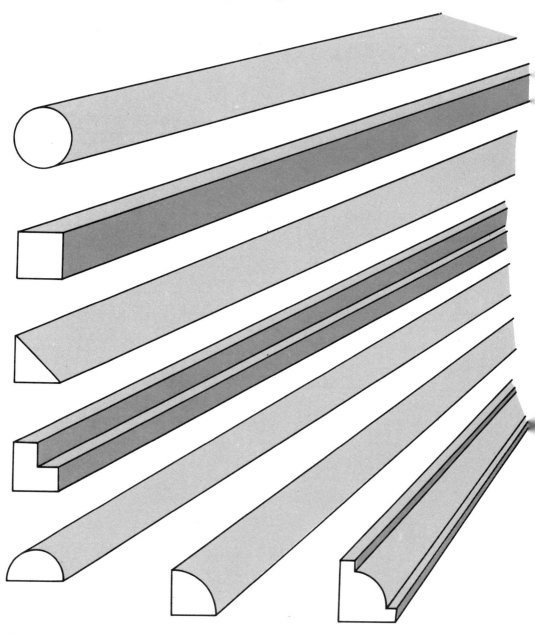

If we cut off a length from any of these strips, we get a solid called a **prism**. We can use the cross-section to name the prism.

Here for example is a **square prism**.

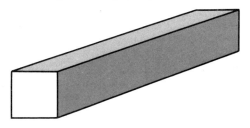

Square prism

The cuts at the ends must be made at right-angles to the length, like this, **not** like this.

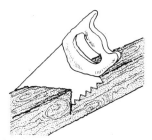
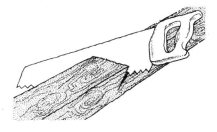

The cross-section of a prism does not have to be one of the shapes shown on the opposite page.

It could be a hexagon, or any shape.

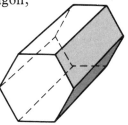

But the cross-section does have to be exactly the same shape and size all the way through.

So this is a prism.

But this is not. (The cross-section gets bigger as you go down the solid.)

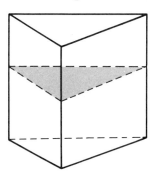
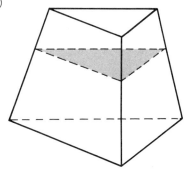

A1 Say whether each of these solids is a prism or not.
Write 'yes' or 'no' for each one.

(a)

(b)

(c)

(d)

(e)

(f)

(g)

(h)

(i)

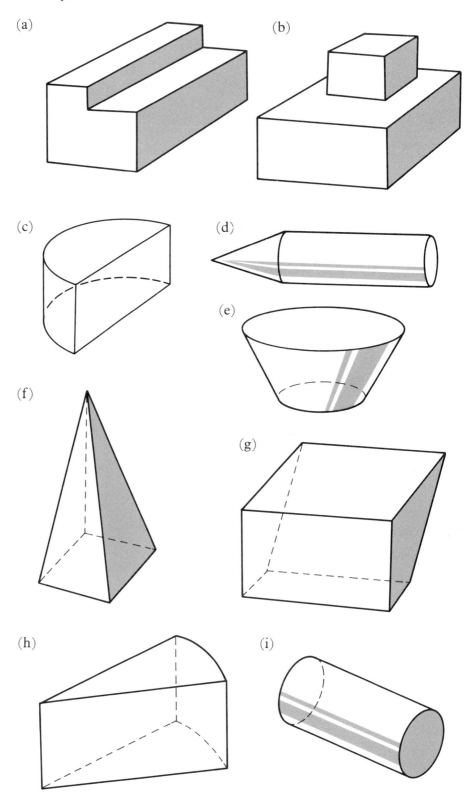

A2 Draw a sketch to show what shape this box will be when it is folded and stuck.

What is the name for the shape of the box?

This flap is glued.

B Volume of a prism

This prism is made from cubes.
Each cube is 1 cm by 1 cm by 1 cm.

The volume of each cube is **1 cubic cm**,
or **1 cm³**.

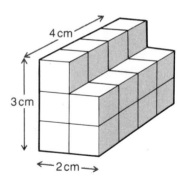

We can find the volume of the prism
by splitting it up into 'layers' along
its length.

5 cubes in
each layer

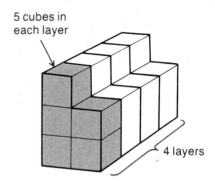

One layer contains 5 cubes.

There are 4 of these layers (because
the prism is 4 cm long).

So the volume of the prism is

$$5 \times 4 = 20\,\text{cm}^3.$$

B1 Find the volume of each of these prisms.
Think of each one as split up into layers.
(Each cube in the diagrams is 1 cm by 1 cm by 1 cm.)

(a)

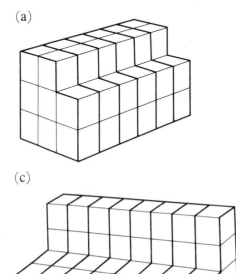

(b)

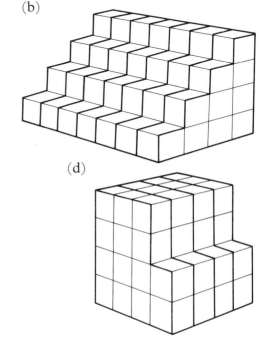

(c)

(d)

Look at this prism.

The area of its cross-section is $7\,\text{cm}^2$.

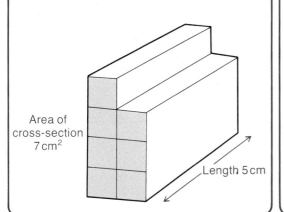

Area of cross-section $7\,\text{cm}^2$

Length 5 cm

The area of the cross-section also tells us how many cubes there are in each layer: 7 cubes.

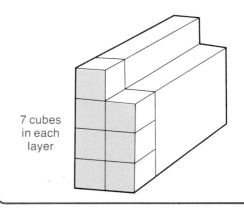

7 cubes in each layer

The length of the prism, 5 cm, tells us how many layers there are.

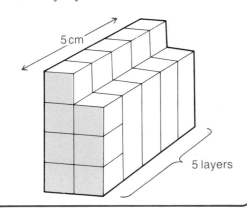

5 cm

5 layers

To find the volume of the prism, we multiply 7 by 5.

We can think of this as multiplying the **area of the cross-section** by the **length**.

Volume of prism =

Area of cross-section × Length

If the area is in cm^2 and the length in cm, the volume will be in cm^3.

B2 Calculate the volume of each of these prisms. (All measurements are in cm.)

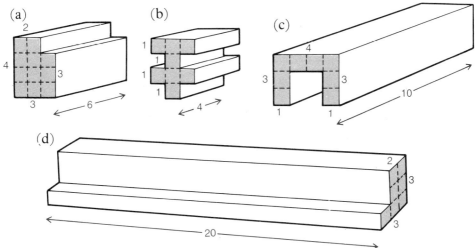

(a)
2
4
3
3
6

(b)
1
1
1
4

(c)
4
3
3
1
1
10

(d)
20
2
3
3

71

The formula 'Volume = Area of cross-section × Length' is true for all prisms, whatever the shape of their cross-section.

B3 (a) The cross-section of this prism is a right-angled triangle. Calculate its area.

(b) Calculate the volume of the prism.

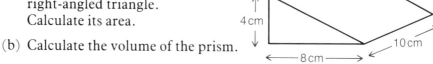

B4 This is a net of a triangular prism, with tabs for sticking.

(a) Draw the net, cut it out and make the prism.

(b) Calculate the volume of the prism.

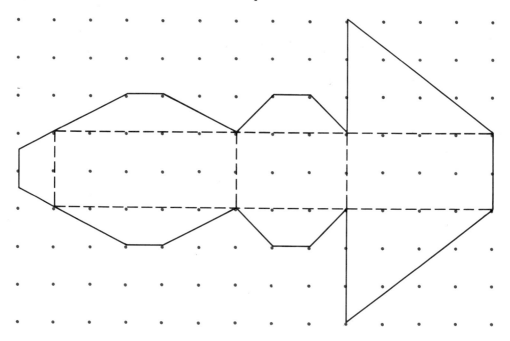

If the area of the cross-section is in m² and the length in m, then the volume will be in m³.

B5 A pool for dolphins has an area of 1430 m². The water is 5·5 m deep everywhere.

Calculate the volume of water in the pool.

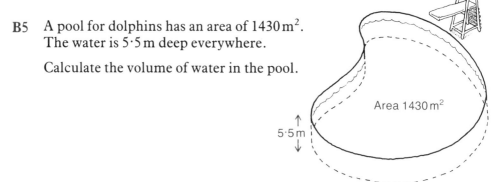

Area 1430 m²

5·5 m

B6 This is a scale drawing of the cross-section of a tunnel.

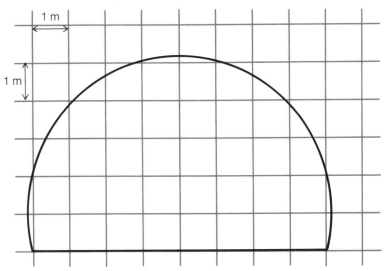

(a) Estimate the area of the cross-section of the tunnel, in m^2.

(b) The tunnel is 476 metres long.
Estimate the volume of the tunnel, in m^3.

(This information would be important to someone designing a ventilating system for the tunnel.)

*Thin prisms

Prisms can be very thin. Instead of 'length' we have 'thickness'.
A piece of cut-out cardboard is a prism, . . .   and so is a patch of oil or paint
(if it is the same thickness all over).

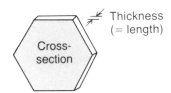

*B7   A piece of pastry covers an area of 650 cm^2 and is 0·4 cm thick.
Calculate its volume.

*B8   In a cake factory, a machine covers the top of each cake
with icing. If the area of the top of the cake is 350 cm^2
and the icing is 0·6 cm thick, calculate the volume of icing.

*B9   A kitchen whose area is 18·5 m^2 has a concrete floor.
The concrete is 0·15 m thick all over.
Calculate the volume of the concrete, to the nearest m^3.

*B10 What volume of sand is needed to fill this sand-pit level with the top? (Find the volume in m³. To do this you will need to change the depth into metres.)

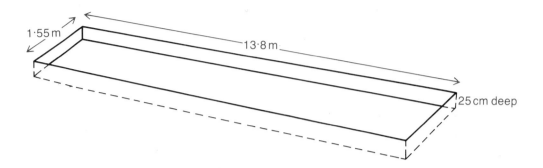

1·55 m

13·8 m

25 cm deep

*B11 This is the plan of a garden.

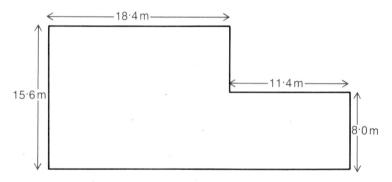

18·4 m

11·4 m

15·6 m

8·0 m

(a) Calculate the area of the garden, in m².

(b) The owner wants to remove top-soil from the garden to a depth of 20 cm all over the garden.

Calculate the volume of top-soil to be removed, to the nearest m³.

*B12 Dawn is going to make a frame for a picture. She cannot decide whether to have glass in front of the picture or not.

If she does use glass, she will need a rectangular piece 59 cm by 45 cm. The glass is 0·3 cm thick.

(a) Calculate the volume of the piece of glass.

(b) 1 cm³ of glass weighs 2·6 grams.
How much extra weight will the glass add to the picture frame? Give your answer in grams, to the nearest gram.

(c) Change your last answer to kilograms.
Now round it off to the nearest 0·1 kg.

c Other solids

A prism whose cross-section is a circle is called a **cylinder**.
Objects shaped like a cylinder are called **cylindrical**.

Cylinder

Cylindrical vacuum cleaner

The best-known kind of **pyramid** has a square base.
But a pyramid can have a base of any shape.

Square-based pyramid

Hexagonal-based pyramid

A pyramid with a circular base is called a **cone**.
Objects shaped like a cone are called **conical**.

Cone

Conical flask

The mathematical name for a ball is a **sphere**.
Objects shaped like a sphere are called **spherical**.

Sphere

Spherical balloon

C1 A solid whose faces are all flat, not curved, is called a **polyhedron**.
Which of these solids are **polyhedra**?

(a) Cube   (b) Cuboid   (c) Cylinder

(d) Square-based pyramid   (e) Cone   (f) Triangular prism

(g) Sphere   (h) A prism whose cross-section is a semicircle

C2 Here are two nets for solids. What kind of solid is each one?

(a)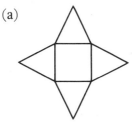

(b)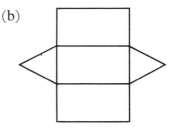

The surface of a sphere is curved all over, 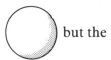 but the

surface of a cone is in two parts, one flat and one curved.
The base is flat, but the rest of the surface is curved.

C3 The curved surface of a cone can be made from a flat piece of paper. Make one yourself, like this.

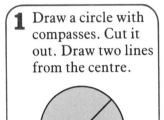

1 Draw a circle with compasses. Cut it out. Draw two lines from the centre.

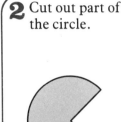

2 Cut out part of the circle.

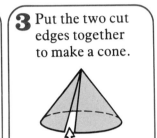

3 Put the two cut edges together to make a cone.

Stick the edges together.

C4 Here are three cones and three nets. Which net belongs to each cone?

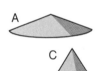

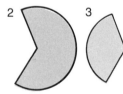

A   B   C   1   2   3

C5 This lampshade is part of a cone. (The top of the cone is missing.)

(a) Draw a rough sketch of what the net for the lampshade looks like.

(b) Draw a net using compasses. Cut it out and make a 'lampshade'.

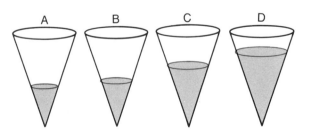

A   B   C   D

C6 Which of these cones do you think is half full? (You can check your guess by making a paper cone and using sand.)

13 In your head (2)

Do these in your head, as quickly as you can.

1. Dawn has 4 boxes of tennis balls. There are 6 balls in each box. How many tennis balls does Dawn have?

2. Write these in figures.

    (a) Four thousand and sixty-nine   (b) Seven thousand and eight

    (c) Eighteen pounds and two pence   (d) Forty pounds and nine pence

3. I bought three cakes, all exactly the same price. The total cost was £2·40. How much did each cake cost?

4. A bag of flour weighs 2 kg. A bag of sugar weighs 750 grams. What is the total weight of the two bags, in grams?

5. Write these as percentages.

    (a) $\frac{1}{4}$ (b) $\frac{3}{10}$ (c) $\frac{9}{10}$ (d) $\frac{53}{100}$ (e) $\frac{3}{4}$

6. I am saving up to buy a clarinet. It costs £75. So far I have saved £48. How much more have I got to save?

7. What is the circumference, roughly, of a circle whose diameter is 2 cm?

8. Work these out.

    (a) 25% of £80   (b) 50% of £680   (c) 75% of £40   (d) 10% of £85

9. Before sunset the temperature was 4 °C. After sunset it had fallen by 7 degrees. What was the temperature after sunset?

10. I bought 5 kg of flour. I used 250 g of it to make a cake. How much did I have left afterwards?

11. Change each of these measurements to metres.

    (a) 5 km   (b) 4·3 km   (c) 0·8 km   (d) 21·3 km   (e) 0·65 km

12. Work these out.

    (a) 25 × 3   (b) 24 × 4   (c) 18 × 5   (d) 17 × 6   (e) 23 × 4

13. Work these out.   (a) $\frac{40}{8}$ (b) $\frac{27}{3}$ (c) $\frac{36}{4}$ (d) $\frac{40}{5}$ (e) $\frac{164}{2}$

14 Plans and elevations

A Getting measurements from drawings

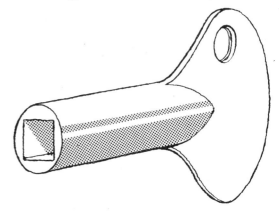

This is a drawing of a key for winding up an old-fashioned clock.

Suppose you wanted someone to make a key just like this one. You would need to give accurate measurements. If a key is not made accurately, it will not fit.

But you cannot get accurate measurements from the drawing. For example, how do you measure the diameter of the shaft?

Is it this . . . 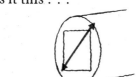 or this . . . or this?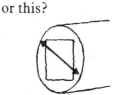

The drawing above is of no use for measurement. A locksmith would need to have **views** of the key, drawn full size or to scale.

Here is a side view of the key, also called a **side elevation**. It is drawn full size here.

A

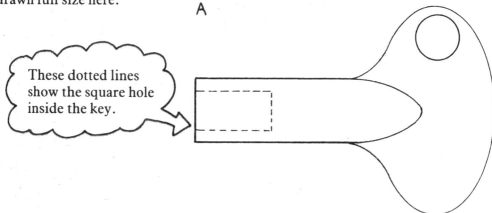

These dotted lines show the square hole inside the key.

This is an end view, or **end elevation**, of the key.

This is a top view, also called a **plan view**.

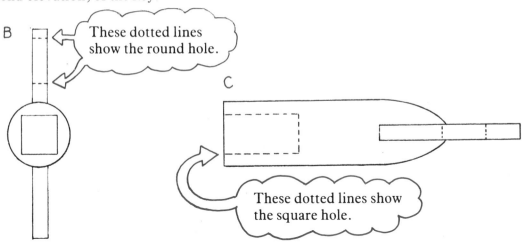

B

These dotted lines show the round hole.

C

These dotted lines show the square hole.

A1 Which of the three drawings, A, B, C, can you measure to find out each of these? (Sometimes you can use more than one drawing.)

Measure them and write down the measurements.

(a) The diameter of the shaft of the key

(b) The depth of the square hole

(c) The diameter of the round hole

(d) The overall length of the key

A2 These are full size drawings of a well-known object.
One is a plan view, the other is a side elevation.

Measure the drawings and draw **full size** an end elevation.
Write the measurements on your drawing.

CAMERA PUZZLE

A3 *You need worksheet B4–6.*
These are drawings of **four** old-fashioned cameras.
There is a plan view, a front elevation and a side elevation of
each camera. All the drawings are to the same scale.

You have to decide which drawings go together and belong to the same
camera. You may need to measure. Use the worksheet for recording
your measurements.

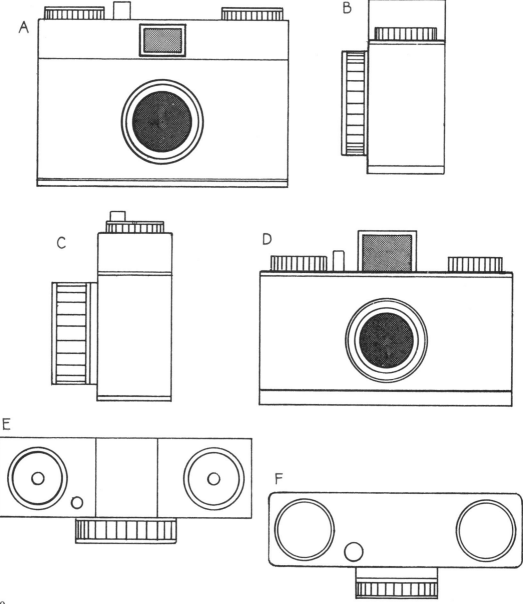

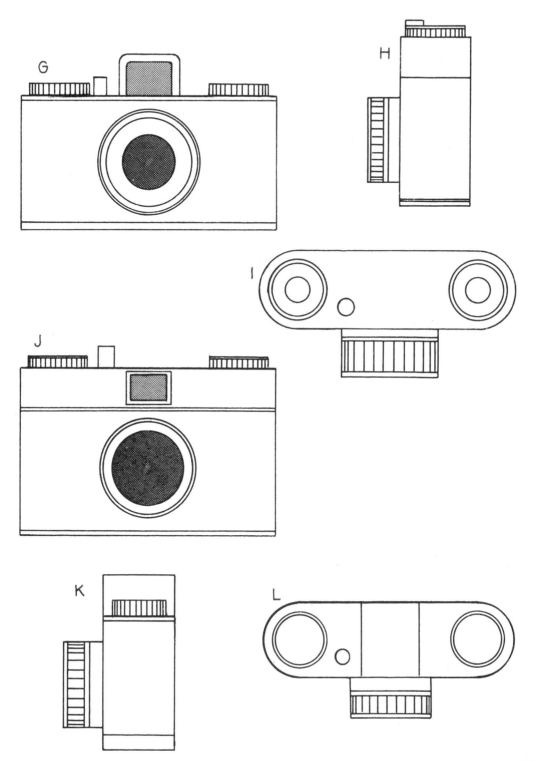

A4 Hema's little sister has seven wooden blocks, all different shapes. Hema put them on a table, and then drew a plan view, a front elevation and a side elevation for each block.

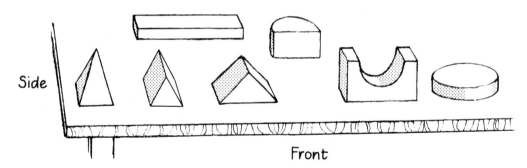

Hema made all her drawings full size. They are shown below and on the next page. They have got muddled up.

Put the drawings into groups of three. Each group will contain the plan and two elevations of one of the seven blocks.
Start by picking out the seven plan views. After that you will need to measure carefully to decide some of the drawings.

A

B

C

D

E

F

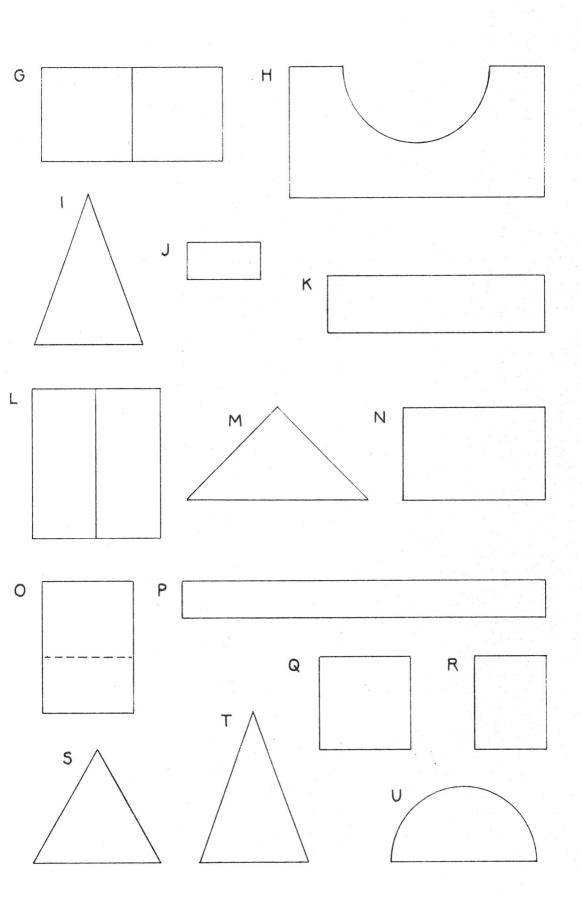

B Buildings

Plans and elevations are often used to give information about the measurements of buildings.

B1 These drawings show a rough sketch of a building, together with a plan view and a side elevation.

The plan and the elevation are drawn to a scale of 1 cm to 1 m.

Plan
view

Side
elevation

(a) Which of the two views do you use to measure the width of the building?

(b) Measure the drawing to find the width in metres.

(c) Use one of the views to find the height in metres of each side wall.

(d) Use one of the views to find the overall height of the building.

(e) Use your answers to make a scale drawing of the end wall of the building. (The end wall is coloured in the sketch.)

(f) From your scale drawing, measure the length of the sloping edge of each part of the roof.

(g) Calculate the total area of the roof of the building in m², to 1 d.p.

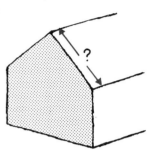

Plan
view

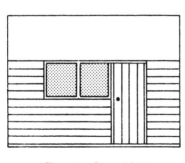

B2 These views of a shed are drawn to a scale of 1 cm to 1 m.

Front elevation

End elevation

Take measurements from the drawings and calculate the area of each of these in m², to 1 d.p.
(a) The floor of the shed   (b) The roof   (c) One end wall

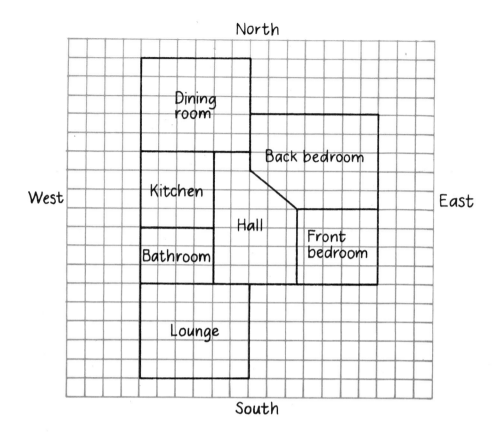

North

West   East

Dining room

Back bedroom

Kitchen

Hall

Front bedroom

Bathroom

Lounge

South

B3   The drawing above shows the ground plan of a bungalow.

(a) On the opposite page there are four elevations of the bungalow. Which of them do you see when you look at the bungalow from the north?

(b) Which do you see when you look from the west?

(c) When the artist drew elevation D, he forgot to draw the chimney. Draw a rough sketch to show where it should be drawn.

(d) How many windows are there in the front bedroom?

(e) These drawings show the insides of four of the rooms. Which room is in each drawing?

(i)   (ii)   (iii)   (iv)

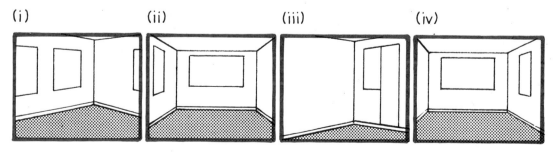

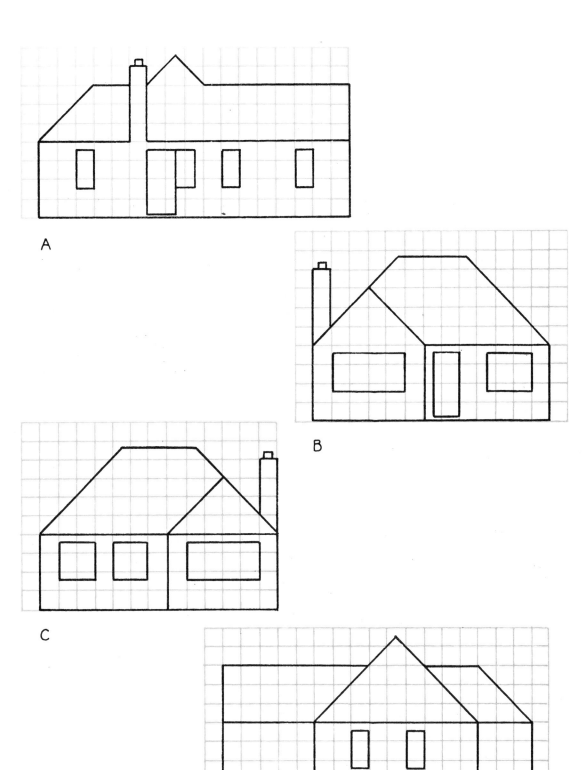

A

B

C

D

15 On paper (2)

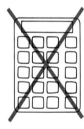

Do these calculations on paper (or in your head if you can) **without using a calculator.**

Try to do them as quickly as you can.

1 A bus company normally has 532 drivers at work, but this week 185 of them are either sick or on holiday.
How many drivers are at work this week?

2 A shop sells a skirt for £8·75 and a blouse for £4·85, but if you buy both you get the pair for £12·50.
How much do you save by buying them together instead of separately?

3 A furniture shop sells a table and four chairs for £88.
The table by itself costs £45. How much do you pay for each chair when you buy the table and chairs?

4 I can get six photos on each page of my photo album.
Altogether I have 36 full pages of photos. How many photos is that?

5 I have to do a business trip from Exeter to Liverpool to Birmingham and back to Exeter.
From Exeter to Liverpool is 235 miles, from Liverpool to Birmingham is 90 miles, and from Birmingham to Exeter is 162 miles.

How far have I got to travel altogether?

6 Sandra was paid £20·70 for 6 hours' work.
How much was that per hour?

7 If you can get 5 glasses of wine from one bottle, how many bottles will you need in order to give 85 people 2 glasses each?

8 A shop sells films at £2·88 each, or £16·50 for six.

(a) How much do you save by buying six films together instead of separate▶

(b) What does each film cost when you buy six together?

9 A garage charges £13·50 per hour for labour. What is the labour cost of a repair which took 7 hours to do?

10 I have read 173 pages of a book which has 308 pages altogether.
How many more pages have I got to read?

Review 3

12 Solids

12.1 Which of these are drawings of prisms?

A  B  C 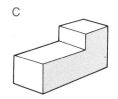 D 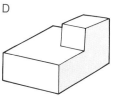 E

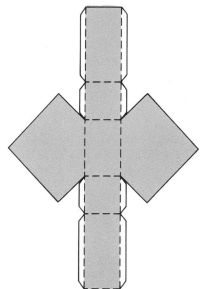

12.2 (a) Draw a sketch of the solid you will get if you cut out the net on the left, fold it and stick it together, using the tabs.

(b) Is the solid a prism?

12.3 Calculate the volume of the solids below. All dimensions are in cm.

(a) 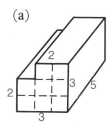 (b)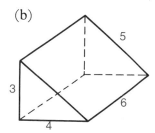

13 In your head (2)

Do these in your head, as quickly as you can.

13.1 (a) 4×16 (b) $55 + 36$ (c) 70×5 (d) $46 \div 10$ (e) 10×0.83

13.2 A customer's total bill came to £4·73. The customer decided that she did not want one of the items after all. That item cost 28p. What did her bill come to when the cost of that item was taken off?

13.3 Estimate the length of this line, in centimetres.

14 Plans and elevations

14.1 There are six different radios shown here. There is a plan view, a front elevation and a side elevation of each one.

Say which views go together as views of the same radio.

14.2 These are drawings of a simple cucumber frame. The shaded part is glass. The scale of the drawings is 1 cm to 10 cm.

Work out the area of the glass.

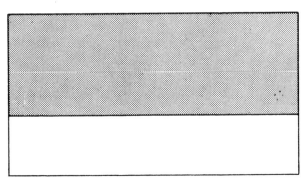

Side elevation   Front elevation

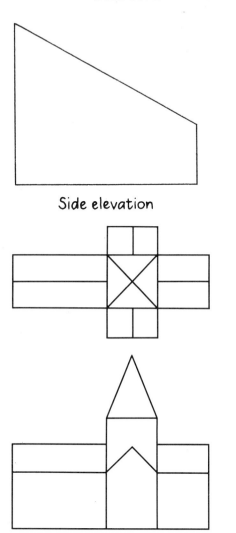

14.3 These drawings show a plan view and a side elevation of a model church.

Sketch an end elevation (left-hand end).

15 On paper (2)

Do these without using a calculator.

    15.1 To hire a tent costs £8·40 for the first 7 days, and then £1·75 a day afterwards.
I want to hire a tent for 10 days. How much will it cost?

    15.2 A garden spade costs £8·65 and a fork costs £7·95. If you buy the two together, you can have them both for £15·75.
How much do you save by buying them together instead of separately?

15.3   Chris bought a car for £375. It needed repairing, so he repaired it himself. He had to buy a new clutch which cost £33·80. He then sold the car for £850. How much did he make?

15.4   Jane takes a film to a shop to have it processed. The shop charges £1·75 for developing the film and an extra 7p for each print. There are 36 pictures on the roll of film. How much will it cost altogether for developing and printing?

M   Miscellaneous

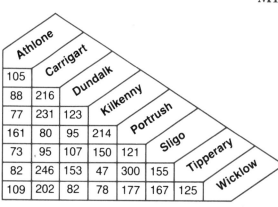

M1   This chart shows the distance in miles between eight towns in Ireland.

    (a)   Which two towns are furthest apart?

    (b)   Which two are closest together?

    (c)   Bernadette lives at Sligo. Each month she makes these trips:

         1 trip to Carrigart and back
         1 trip to Dundalk and back
         2 trips to Wicklow and back

      What distance is that altogether?

M2   (a)   Measure angles a and b and write down their sizes.

    (b)   The straight lines l and m eventually meet. What will the angle be between l and m?

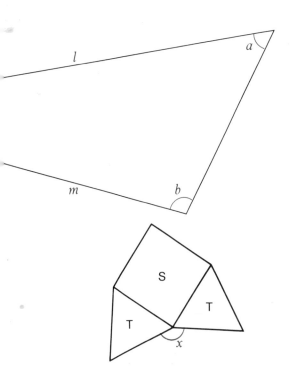

M3   S is a square and each T is an equilateral triangle.

    Calculate the angle marked x, showing your working.